SAD!

DONALD 'BIFF' TRUMP
IS PRESIDENT

The strange similarities
between Donald Trump
and bully Biff Tannen
from *Back to the Future II*

By Paul Orwell, a nobody

Copyright © 2018

SAD! Donald 'Biff' Trump Is President

Oceania Press
paul@paulorwell.com

ISBN-13: 978-0692183571
ISBN-10: 0692183574

Printed in the United States of America

RAINN

800-656-HOPE (4673)

24/7 online chat – rainn.org

Find help and the resources you need.

RAINN (Rape, Abuse & Incest National Network)
is the nation's largest anti-sexual violence organization.
RAINN created and operates the
National Sexual Assault Hotline 800-656-HOPE (4673)

BACK TO THE FUTURE

Biff the Original and 'Biff' the President

BIFF TANNEN, THE BEEFY BULLY from the *Back to the Future* movie trilogy, and Donald J. Trump are the same man living in different times and different realities. One lives in the 1980s movie franchise, one lives in the White House. They are time-twins. The same man. The Biff Tannen casino owner character in the *Back to the Future Part II* time-travel scenarios was even based on Donald Trump. Google it!

Skip to the next chapter if you want to dig in and explore the stunning similarities between Biff Tannen and Donald Trump, from their hair to their height to their harems. I'm going to take a moment here to set the context and explain why there's a serious reason beyond the laughs to compare them. If that's not for you, take your DeLorean and zoom straight to Chapter 2 at 88 miles per hour.

Let's start with a couple of quotes about the future:

"I try to learn from the past but I plan for the future by focusing exclusively on the present. That's where the fun is."

and

"Learn from yesterday, live for today, hope for tomorrow. The important thing is to not stop questioning."

The first quote doesn't seem to fully grasp the past, has a hazy vision of the future, and focuses on fun today. It was spoken by Donald J. Trump, or "Biff" Trump as I refer to him in this book. "Biff" Trump is a low-IQ hustler who was and is an extremely good self-promoter, possibly the best in history. Right now, he happens to be president of the United States. Like a bull in a china shop, he will leave the store with a snort and with shards of broken saucers all over the floor without recognizing the damage he did.

The second quote understands that time is an interconnected continuum and stresses hope and perpetual questioning. It is optimistic and civil. They are the words of Albert Einstein (Einstein is also the name of Doc Brown's dog in *Back to the Future*.) Einstein, the man, was a genius who knew more about the nature of time than anyone. Biff Tannen is no genius and "Biff" Trump is no Einstein; they can't fathom time beyond the moment and have the attention span of a goldfish.

Whether we like it or not, none of us can escape our past – we are connected to it and a product of it – but our future is ours to make of it what we will. We might want to change things in our past ... but we can't. We might want to get a glimpse of the future and see what's comin' ... but we can't do that either. But in the movies WE CAN! In the beloved films of *Back to the Future*, we travel with Marty McFly as he goes back to the past or forward into the future, making changes that disrupt the space-time continuum.

Along the way Marty bumps into bad guy Biff Tannen, who tangles with him in 1985, 1955, 2015, in a 1985 alternate reality in which Biff has become rich and powerful, 1955 (again), and in 1885 where the bully character is represented by Biff's great-grandfather Buford "Mad Dog" Tannen. In each movie, in all timelines, in every version of Biff, we see a cardboard cut-out and stand-in for Donald Trump. In *Back to the Future Part II* (or BTTF2, as it's later abbreviated), the screenwriter used Trump as the inspiration for Biff's character in the movie's alternate 1985 timeline.

There are many superficial examinations of these time-twins available to read online (check out the additional reading list provided at the end of this book), but this book will consider larger questions, too, such as "What does it mean for us that we elected Biff Tannen as president of the United States?" and "Why?"

The chapters are self-contained so you can skip among them like Doc Brown skips through time. We'll start with the basics: the similarities in their looks, lifestyles, and livelihoods; the hair, the casinos, the penthouses. We'll look at their bullying ways, from signature taunts to aggressive behavior, then examine how the Biffs treat women and how they talk about them. We'll also compare them as businessmen; both men see business (and life) as a zero-sum game, so in order to win, someone else has to lose.

We'll also consider how the Biffs relate to small-town America. Biff Tannen lives in Hill Valley, then runs it, and turns it into "Hell" Valley. "Biff" Trump maintains a pretense of care for the communities in the heartland, but he is, in fact, corrupting them too. If "Biff" Trump could make it so, miners in West Virginia would be digging coal into the 2030s even after the rest of the world switched to cheaper and greener electricity.

We'll also explore whether and how the Trump problem could be fixed if we had a DeLorean and could zip back into the past. Maybe time travel is why we have what we have today – could the Russians or Trump himself have already tried it?

Finally, in the words of that timeless phrase from Ronald Reagan's 1980 presidential campaign, we'll consider what it will take to "Make America Great Again."

✳

I want to clearly state that I am not anti-Republican; I am anti-liar and anti-bully, regardless of a person's political persuasion. I am anti-fraud, anti-arrogance, and anti-vanity. I am for fairness, transparency, and intelligence – and I believe that politicians should have heart, empathy, and soul. These things are absent in our current president, who rides roughshod over political convention, common sense, and basic decency. Far from being a great deal-maker, he has polarized Congress to an extraordinary degree. Compromise or even conversation between our two great parties is harder now than ever. If we needed a principled leader, we got a wheeler-dealer instead.

WHY? WHY ME? WHY NOW?

I went to a Donald Trump rally the night before he was elected in 2016. There was a positive feeling in the air; the rowdy auditorium was filled with good people, men and women, veterans, hopeful folks in high spirits. These weren't deplorables, they were people like you and me. Rudy's wind-up speech got the crowd quite revved up before the main event. At this late stage, we were all familiar with Donald's shtick and soundbites: pointing to the "fake news" at the back of the room, praising the "incredible movement" gathered in the auditorium, promising a "big beautiful wall" on the border with Mexico. By then there was a sense that certain things might *actually* be possible even though, later, in the cold light of a Maryland morning, I realized it was unlikely that a single person could in fact "drain the swamp." But I was drawn in, I wanted to be there, and I *wanted* to believe "Biff" was different, even though I half-suspected that the poacher had simply turned gamekeeper.

Now, two years later, the dream has turned to dust and the emperor has no clothes. We see the man's basest animal instincts all too clearly. America hasn't seen the manufacturing boom "Biff" promised, though you can be sure that will be touted again if he runs in 2020. There is no wall. From a diplomat's perspective, we are the laughingstock of nations around the world. Luckily for us, the economy is doing well and continuing to follow its meandering rise from the depths of the recession in 2008. "Biff" hasn't fouled that up. Yet.

The midterms are upon us and they give us a chance to stand up and vote. That's my goal: to add my voice to the chorus singing and shouting "No! No more Biff!"

This isn't a book about Republicans versus Democrats. It's about all Americans and that's why I chose the American flag for the book's cover with its equal portions of red and blue. This flag is upside down, an international symbol of distress, because I'm deeply distressed by the quality and tone of our current political discourse.

There are countless books on our boy Donald, both praising and pummeling him – everyone's got a personal point of view. I chose to compare Trump to a character that we've all known for 30 years, Biff Tannen from the *Back to the Future* movies. Biff Tannen is that rare character we all have a clear and unified view of: he's the bad guy! He's an asshole!

We want our president – no matter who it is – to be a great leader. Many movies and video games stress the importance of the star, the single person who gets the job done. In reality, though, even a strong leader needs a strong team to effect change, to make things happen, to achieve consensus and get things done.

Biff could run Hill Valley and "Hell" Valley with the help of his three dumb cronies, but the United States can't be run that way.

Yes, a leader needs to lead, but a leader must also cajole, persuade, beg, and compromise. That's how you get your people *and* those other people to agree, consent, or acquiesce. Biff Tannen didn't need to: he could rule by fiat. That's how "Biff" Trump ran the Trump Organization, but now that he's in politics, that's not gonna fly. To get both the Senate and House of Representatives to move in the same direction is difficult and complicated. The give-and-take sometimes involves crowds of people sitting around working to hammer out a compromise.

In the movies it's so simple. As Biff Tannen watches TV from his penthouse hot tub (BTTF2), he sees the "Man With No Name" (Clint Eastwood's role in *A Fistful of Dollars*) dispense justice swiftly and shoot Ramon Rojo dead. In BTTF3, "Mad Dog" Tannen is the gun-toting villain. But the idea that merely pulling a trigger can solve problems is for simpletons. It's as idiotic as Biff Tannen showing up at the White House and being given nuclear codes or being placed in charge of the nation's schools. He can't! He's an idiot, a bully, and wholly self-centered. Asking corrupt Biff Tannen from BTTF2 to regulate business would simply lead to massive tax breaks for the industries that benefit him; he can't help himself and doesn't know any better. Expecting the boor to envision race or sex equality would be absurd: in the movie he calls George

McFly an "Irish bug" and repeatedly tries to molest Lorraine.

SO LET'S GET INTO IT ... It is said that history repeats itself and that the past is the future. Maybe. Take a read and I hope it makes you think about the candidates' character and who you vote for when you next put an X in the box by a name.

LOOK-ALIKES

Tall, big and rich, and assholes

DONALD TRUMP IS A LOT LIKE BIFF Tannen, the bad guy throughout the *Back to the Future* trilogy, but in BTTF2 there are so many parallels between the two it's just plain weird. The men look alike physically, both are wealthy, they share a fondness for flashy women and flashier penthouses, and each has owned casinos. It's particularly weird when you consider how long ago BTTF2 was conceived. Bob Gale started writing the screenplay for this second movie in 1986, although principal photography didn't begin until February 1989.

Search the internet for "Donald Trump Biff Tannen" and you'll see thousands of headlines like these:

How Back To The Future 2's Alternate Timeline Basically Predicted Donald Trump[1]

'Back to the Future' Writer: Biff Is Donald Trump[2]

Believe it: 'Back to the Future' predicted Trump's run[3]

Look at the images in the search results and compare Biff and Trump side-by-side. Flip to the back of this book to the appendix "See for Yourself" to compare how alike their verbal bluster and boasts are. Weird!

And it's no coincidence. Bob Gale, the screenwriter and producer, revealed in a 2015 interview that the then-young Donald Trump had inspired the character of Biff Tannen in BTTF2's 1985 alternate reality, saying,

Yeah. That's what we were thinking about.[4]

One's a real prick, the other's an unreal prick. No coincidence.

Yes, way back in the 1980s, New York's "brash new landlord" was already making a name for himself. In May 1984, Donald "Biff" Trump was featured on the cover of *GQ* magazine with a story titled "Success. How Sweet It Is. Men Who Take Risks and Make Millions."[5] Trump's legend took firm root when his book *The Art of the Deal* (co-authored with Tony Schwartz) was released to much fanfare on November 1, 1987. It rose to the number-one spot on *The New York Times* Best Sellers list and held the lead for 13 weeks.

Decades later, on the very same day that Vice President Joe Biden announced he would not run for president, an interview revealing that Trump inspired Biff was published in observance of "Back to the Future Day" (October 21, 2015).[6] The exclusive generated an incredible volume of media

✳

coverage, most of which reported mainly on the superficial and financial similarities between the two look-alikes.

They're big guys, tall – both 6 foot 3 inches – and heavyset. (We'll look at how they throw that weight around in the next chapter.) They both flaunt golden clouds of hair and Biff sports an iconic style much like Trump's.

While it doesn't much matter how long a casino owner spends on his coif, it's a tad concerning that the president of the United States devotes more time to his hair than to reading his briefing papers. A different president might start the day studying combat-readiness reports; Trump prefers to spend hours each morning watching Fox News while his personal hairdresser wields a comb, hairspray, and mirror to sculpt his locks.[7]

Both are paper billionaires with a history of involvement in the casino business. Consider Biff Tannen's Pleasure Paradise – the tallest building in the city in BTTF2, with "HOTEL RESORT CASINO GIRLS" in flashing lights. Biff's name is emblazoned in huge letters over the entrance, which has red carpet running up the stairs – the very image of a Trump resort property.

Biff's a wealthy man, and like Trump, he's not modest about it. Check out the front of his casino, where there's a huge image of his smiling face as he lights a cigar using a fistful of burning $100 bills.

And Biff himself? We find him ensconced at the top of the building, where he reigns over his kingdom from an opulent penthouse – much like Trump did from his Trump Tower residence before he moved to 1600 Pennsylvania Avenue. Take a look inside the penthouse to get a taste of Biff Tannen's "taste." The penthouse is glitzy, gilded, and over-the-top, filled with animal-skin finishes and flashy furnishings.

Marty McFly confronts Biff in the inner sanctum of this penthouse – his office. Biff's desk is banked on both sides by multiple TV surveillance screens and behind it hangs the *pièce de résistance*: a portrait of Biff. As Biff stands in front of his portrait, it seems to be more than just *reminiscent* of Trump posing with one of *his* own portraits – it's so very Trumpian, it appears that it's actually *meant to be* Trump.[8]

To some, such a display of wealth is glamorous; it might even be called aspirational design. To others, it's gaudy, ostentatious, even tacky – a faux Versailles. Writer Peter York has a name for this specific style, calling it "dictator chic." He says Trump "would fit right in" with your average autocrat's design sensibilities.[9] The dictator chic design aesthetic is fascinatingly out of line with both America's past and present. Everything is big, fake, gold, and glass. Pause for a split-second to consider the fact that when Mahatma Gandhi died, he had fewer than 10 possessions, including a watch and two sandals. Enough said.

FAT CHANCE!

The Measure of the Man

B IFF TANNEN DOES NOT EXAGGERATE his height or weight in *Back to the Future*. He doesn't need to. He's nearly always the tallest and strongest guy in the room. "Biff" Trump, on the other hand, lies about both.

The report of Trump's first presidential physical exam in January 2018 officially states he's 6 foot 3 and 239 pounds, yet a quick web search turns up his driver's license, which clearly shows his height as being only 6 foot 2. Compare photographs of Trump standing next to Canadian Prime Minister Justin Trudeau, who is indeed 6 foot 3, and we see that Trudeau clearly is taller.[10]

So what's an inch one way or another? A back-of-the-envelope calculation shows that Trump is only two pounds or half an inch away from being clinically classified as "obese" (defined as having a body mass index of 30.0 or higher), rather than merely overweight. Based on the height stated on Trump's driver's license, he *is* obese. We all know it's far easier to lie about weight; do you "kinda maybe" think that the White House physician Ronny Jackson might have shaved a couple of pounds off Trump's weight during his first presidential physical? You betcha! So, Trump qualifies as obese on each metric and taken together, he definitely meets the definition.

The point, though, is not whether he's 6 foot 3 or just 6 foot 2 or whether he weighs in at 239 or is more like 280. The point is that he lies about it. Repeatedly.

Let me be clear: I am not making a judgment on a person's weight or on obesity; I am making a point about honesty. I don't care whether someone is as thin as a rail or as big as a house. I care about truthfulness – and you'll find little of that in the health statement submitted on behalf of candidate Trump by his long-time personal physician. In a December 2015 letter, Dr. Harold Bornstein wrote, "If elected, Mr. Trump, I can state unequivocally, will be the healthiest individual ever elected to the presidency."

You can't make this stuff up.

He did it because Trump told him to, even though it was patently absurd. In fact, Bornstein later admitted that Trump had dictated the letter to him.[11]

If Trump didn't repeatedly exaggerate his vigor, strength, and physical prowess, I wouldn't mention his lard-like sagging body. I wouldn't find fault with President William Howard Taft, who weighed over 350 pounds on the day of his inauguration over 100 years ago. But I do find fault with Trump – because of his vanity, self-aggrandizement, and pretense.

"Biff" Trump lies about his height and weight, which are quite clearly *visible*. He boasts that he'll be the healthiest president ever, yet instead of healthful pursuits, he has a fondness for fast foods and watches TV much of the day. If he lies about the visible, we can be darned sure that he's also lying about his invisible opinions and emotions. We can be certain that he's lying about his activities and involvement with Stormy Daniels (but who cares?), his net worth (if we care), and his collusion with Russia around election hacking (we certainly should care).

"Biff" Trump lies about everything, when he isn't lying around; our "tanning bed" president has goggles on and eyes shut.

By contrast, Biff Tannen doesn't lie. He's just a bully. In BTTF2, when Marty McFly confronts him about *Gray's Sports Almanac*, Biff owns up to it (and then tries to shoot Marty). He's also clearly athletic, unlike "Biff" Trump. In BTTF3, the Tannen character is an excellent horseback rider, a good shot, and handy with a lasso, too (roping Marty before attempting to hang him).

President Taft did not hide from his obesity. He sought – and followed – medical advice to address concerns about his health and weight. He hired diet experts and a physical trainer, and he exercised regularly – including riding horseback. Donald

✳

Trump does not ride horses; he rides golf carts and escalators.

Sean Spicer has described "Biff" Trump as a person "riding a unicorn across a rainbow." I disagree. I do not think Donald would be able to even mount a unicorn; if he succeeded, though, I doubt he'd be able to ride it without killing it – or falling off with a very loud thud.

Third time's a charm

Donald "Biff" Trump is now married to his third wife, Melania. In BTTF2's 1985 alternate timeline, Hill Valley has become "Hell" Valley and Biff Tannen is married to wife number three – Lorraine ("third time's a charm," he declares). Lorraine climbs the penthouse stairs decked out in a glittering evening gown and dripping with jewels as if representing "Hell" Valley in one of Trump's once-famous beauty pageants ... if only she were smiling instead of drinking. When Lorraine stands at the top of the stairs, the paintings behind her of women in lingerie (portraits of Lorraine?) call to mind the many photos of Trump over the years with scantily-clad models.

Both men have mean streaks: In BTTF2, Biff threatens to cut off not only Lorraine, but also her children, saying "Your idiot son, Dave, I'll get his parole revoked. And as for Marty, well, maybe you'd like all three of your kids behind bars." And in real life we have "Biff" Trump ridiculing Gold Star parents who were mourning their slain son. How could they do these things?

Both men love money. There's a scene about midway through BTTF2 when Marty peers through the windows of the Biff Tannen Museum and hears narration boasting about Biff's constant winning and wealth.[12] Yet neither Biff nor Trump is truly a self-made man. Biff used *Gray's Sports Almanac,* a sports results book brought back from the future, to make his fortune in the alternate 1985 timeline. But without it, he ends up running a car detailing business. "Biff" Trump was given millions of dollars by his father. Without that head start, who knows what he'd be doing today?

Listen to the difference between Biff's life as a casino owner and the way he pitches himself: Not only is he "one of the richest and most powerful men in America," he's also "Hill Valley's #1 citizen, America's Greatest Living Folk Hero, the one and only Biff Tannen." The hyperbole runs even thicker in deleted footage that didn't make it into the movie's final cut:

"... his charm attracts the most sought-after beauties. His power and influence made him the model of world leaders and heads of state. He was such a tremendous athlete that his high school demanded he repeat his senior year so that the football team would have the benefit of his athletic prowess for an extra season."[13]

Sound like anyone you know? The scene also seems to foretell a future for Biff in politics. For a brief moment, we see footage of Biff on TV. He looks cleaned-up and polished as he speaks into a cluster of media microphones before a cheering crowd. "I just want to say one thing: God bless America."

But in the end, does it even matter whether Biff was intentionally based on Trump?

Probably not. But here's what does matter: they're both examples of a simple stereotype. They're both assholes.

asshole (noun):
a stupid, annoying, or detestable person[14]

While it may be amusing to look at Biff standing in front of his portrait and then gape at the comparisons between Biff Tannen and "Biff" Trump, in reality this is a serious matter: Not only do "Biff" and Biff physically resemble each other, their emotions, intelligence, attitude, and behavior are scarily similar too.

This isn't a movie. We are living this one. In the following chapters, we'll see that both Biffs are mean, abusive men in positions of authority who use their power to bully and compel others. Both are humorless. Both lack empathy and heart. One shapes a town, the other is in charge of a nation.

Donald "Biff" Trump is surely nothing to joke about.

WHAT ARE YOU LOOKING AT, BUTTHEAD?

~ **Biff Tannen,** *Back to the Future* (1985)

BIFF TANNEN IS ONE OF AMERICA'S best-known movie bullies. "Biff" Trump is perhaps America's best-known real bully, now emboldened by the power of the presidency, its megaphone, and the mania of his tweets. Biff and "Biff" are both intellectual simpletons.

The screenplay of BTTF1 describes Biff as "an intimidating lout," and on screen we first meet him in the McFly home, where he is berating Marty's father George McFly.

As Biff looms over George in a display of physical dominance, he uses several of his signature moves. Grabbing George by the shirt, he hammers his head while shouting "Hello? Anybody home? Think, McFly, think!" Moments later, Biff preys on George's naiveté; he points at the floor, George looks down, and Biff cuffs him on the chin. He then grabs candy from a jar, leaves its lid off, and helps himself to a beer from George's fridge while taunting, "all you've got for me is lite beer?"

Biff is at the McFly home to return George's car, which he'd borrowed and wrecked. Rather than apologize or offer to cover the repair costs, Biff invents a reason to blame George for the incident:

"I can't believe you loaned me a car without *telling me it had a blind spot.*"

He's still not done, and in a brazen little cash-grab, Biff shouts "I wanna know who's gonna pay for this" and demands $20 for cleaning his suit, which was stained when beer spilled on it during the car accident.

But he's still not finished. He issues an ultimatum that his reports due at work will be completed by George. In short, Biff Tannen is a flaming asshole and a bully.

He isn't very smart but some of his insults are memorable. "Butthead" is his go-to favorite, though he employs others: loser, dipshit, wiseass, son of a bitch, idiot, chicken, and Irish bug.

"Biff" Trump is also an asshole who can match Biff Tannen barb for barb. "Biff" Trump's insults could fill a phonebook and then some: Lyin' Ted, low-energy Jeb, face of a dog, low IQ, the dumbest man on television ... the list goes on and on and on. The *New York Times* even published a list of "The 487 People, Places, and Things Donald Trump Has Insulted on Twitter."

Bullying comes naturally to the man and he seems to enjoy it as much as Biff Tannen does.

In BTTF2, Biff catches a ball that five little kids are playing with. When they ask for it back, he goads them and then throws the ball onto the roof of a house and laughs at them.

That's the kind of men these Biffs are.

✳

Both Biff Tannen and Donald "Biff" Trump nickel-and-dime the working man, the kind of person who will protest but ultimately not fight a bully. In June 2016, *USA Today* reported that there were hundreds of accusations and liens against "Biff" Trump for unpaid bills, including some from plumbers, waiters, even a dishwasher.[15]

This is reminiscent of the scene in BTTF2 where Biff Tannen argues with the mechanic who repaired his car (and removed a load of horse manure from it). Calling the $302.57 charge "bullshit," Biff makes the outlandish claim that the mechanic probably sold the horseshit for a profit and demands to be compensated! The mechanic gave him four cans of oil.

When regular bullying doesn't work, Biff Tannen simply resorts to physical violence. In BTTF2 he says to Marty, "You wanna take a poke at me?" and proceeds to gut-punch (his stepson) Marty.

Compare this to Donald "Biff" Trump in 2018 when he tweeted this threat at former Vice President Joe Biden:

> *Crazy Joe Biden is trying to act like a tough*
> *guy. Actually, he is weak, both mentally and*
> *physically, and yet he threatens me, for the*

*second time, with physical assault. He
doesn't know me, but he would go down
fast and hard, crying all the way.
Don't threaten people Joe!*[16]

"Biff" Trump waxes nostalgic for the good old days when protesters were "carried out on a stretcher,"[17] when dissent was met by a fist from bullies like Biff Tannen, and when football allowed "a great tackle, a violent head-on tackle."[18]

We live in a democracy where decency is to be applauded. We don't take a fist to an opponent; we use words built into arguments that persuade.

Think of the physical bullying tactics that Donald "Biff" Trump has used to establish physical superiority and intimidate others. During his presidential debates with Hillary Clinton, he prowled around menacingly, like a stalker.[19]

His white-knuckle handshake, known as the "grab and yank," is his signature (much like Biff's knuckle-to-the-head move) though it sometimes backfires.[20] In Italy, at NATO headquarters, Trump pushed past the Prime Minister of Montenegro to get into the camera shot.[21] Observers around the world were appalled.

Both Biffs run by the "take, don't ask" playbook. If we let them get into positions of power, they'll take from us without asking because that's their nature. In school, Marty McFly got close enough to pull Biff off Lorraine in the school cafeteria, and George McFly got close enough to punch him in the face when Biff assaulted Lorraine in the parking lot during the school's "Enchantment Under the Sea" dance.

We don't get the opportunity to punch in politics. Voting, protest, and due process are our remedies.

Remember that the mentality of a bully (or an autocrat) is always about "me." Other people think about "us" (and their "us" includes people who did not vote for them). "Biff" Trump does not care about an America-wide "us." He cares only about his followers' votes and he castigates his opponents. Most politicians in power today know that they'll be in opposition sometime soon so they don't burn bridges – but "Biff" Trump lives in the now, day to day. He doesn't think long-term. When he's done with the presidency, he won't look back or care what's left behind: he'll be back to making money.

Bullies are emboldened by passivity. If we don't punch Biff Tannen in the face, if we don't censure "Biff" Trump in Congress, they get worse because they do not observe established rules of civility and decency. You may enjoy watching a shark rip apart a smaller fish, but if you fall into the tank you should expect to be ripped apart too.

"Low IQ" Donnie

Is Biff Tannen smart? He's cunning, at least in the BTTF2 storyline where Old Biff steals the *Sports Almanac* and delivers it to his younger self. But it takes young Biff over three years to place a bet using the book.

In BTTF2, low-IQ Biff profits at the expense of his community, pursuing business deals in power generation, toxic waste disposal, and gambling. He's rich. He's cunning. He's mean. But he doesn't seem that smart. In BTTF1, low-IQ Biff becomes a car detailer. In BTTF3, his great-grandfather Buford "Mad Dog" Tannen is functionally illiterate and needs help counting: he does not know that seven comes after six.

Similarly, it's hard to find evidence of "Biff" Trump's smarts outside the real estate business: plenty of failures, countless policy contradictions, and more recently, thousands of tweets – a medium perfectly suited to his attention span.

He's rich – that's true – but so was Gary Dahl, the inventor of the pet rock. So, what makes us think a single-minded rich guy can lead a diverse nation of 328 million people?

Ask "Biff" Trump to read a paragraph about a policy position and then describe it. Even if the reading material was grammatically correct, he'd find explanation impossible. Simply impossible. He has the smarts and speech patterns of Archie Bunker. Put him at the despatch box in Parliament in London and there would be peals of laughter from both sides of the House.

The sophistication of his communication was never that high, but it has regressed in recent years as he uses fewer and fewer tools from his toolkit, until only the bluntest remain. Language experts have assessed his words as those used by a child between third and seventh grade.

Besides the *The Art of the Deal*, we never see "Biff" Trump with books; he doesn't read much or at all – not even briefing papers. The only publication ever in Biff Tannen's hands is the *Sports Almanac*. We saw "Biff" Trump's hand on the Bible when he was sworn in, but he can't recite from it or explain what's inside. Instead he watches Fox News.

The bad grammar and misspelled (or misnamed) nouns in "Biff" Trump's tweets echo the mutilated language of the Biffs before him: In BTTF3, great-grandfather Mad Dog Tannen says, "I'll hunt you and shoot you down like a duck" ... instead of a dog. In BTTF1, Biff says "why don't you make like a tree and get out of here" ... instead of leave. In BTTF2, Biff says "that's about as funny as a screen door on a battleship" ... instead of on a submarine.

James 4:6

As president, "Biff" Trump uses his bully pulpit to humiliate those who disagree with him. For those of you who believe in Jesus (no offense if you don't) think for a moment about Jesus' qualities of service, humility, passivity, and love. Every week, followers of Jesus drop to their knees and ask for forgiveness. "Biff" Trump claims to be a Christian but can you imagine him dropping to his knees and asking for forgiveness? He just wouldn't.

In his twisted mind, dropping to one's knees is not an act of penitence or prostration but of humiliation or sexual submission, an ugly pose before dominance and power.

"Biff" Trump said, "I could have told Mitt Romney to drop to his knees," therein deeply insulting Romney, a good family man and a committed Christian.[22] It was surely deliberate, and Romney surely heard it that way. To former Playboy Playmate Brande Roderick on network television, he casually and instinctively mocked her, saying "It must be a pretty picture, you dropping to your knees."[23] Astonishing!

Now imagine a meeting between "Biff" Trump and Jesus. "Biff" would probably grab Jesus' hand and white-knuckle shake it, then diss Jesus for being "weak on crime" and turning the other cheek.

Empty vessels make the most noise

Smart people know there's a lot to know and that they certainly don't know everything. Stupid people never realize that and think they are smarter than they are. So, a smart person will rarely boast about their intellect but a stupid person often will. Sound like anyone you know? Perhaps someone who tweeted that he was:

> *"... like, really smart ...*
> *a very stable genius."*[24]

Since a genius understands how much he doesn't know, he would be unlikely to say such a thing, whereas a bona fide idiot has no clue about what he doesn't know, so he would say it and believe it.

Think about some of the things "Biff" Trump doesn't talk about. We don't hear about meditation, about striking compromises, about bringing sides together, about using tactics of give and take to reconcile differences. We see no evidence of grace; he can't comprehend (or even spell) *noblesse oblige*.

Countless articles have been written about how the audience thought Richard Nixon beat John F. Kennedy in the 1960 presidential debate when they listened on the radio – most called it a draw. People who watched the debate on TV, however, saw a young man with a nice tan, a dark suit, and a big smile – the very picture of a healthy man. Nixon, pale and sweaty and wearing an ill-fitting gray suit, trailed far behind in TV viewers' estimation. Bob Dole later said that Kennedy wiped Nixon out.

What many know about Donald Trump is shaped by television media coverage and what they think they see. That's like oohing and cooing over the path of a shiny pinball, when it's the flippers, bumpers, and gravity that make it move. That bright shiny object isn't so interesting once it has come to rest, fallen out of play.

We in America have lost sight of who the bullies, the bad guys, and the good guys are. The good guys are the productive and constructive members of society whether or not they are famous: the silent and steady contributors, the church-goers, the law-abiders, the salt of the earth. The bad guys are the showy assholes who make the most of media, smiling as they skim and scam. The bullies bang their fists and spray flecks of spittle, banking on the majority of good Americans to keep their heads down and stay out of the way – instead of dumping a load of well-deserved horseshit on them.

Michele Obama said, "When they go low, we go high." For once bully "Biff' Trump agrees with an Obama, though he would turn it around: "When they go high, we go low."

WOMEN: YOU HAVE TO TREAT 'EM LIKE SHIT.

~ Donald Trump, *New York* magazine (November 9, 1992)

DONALD TRUMP, THE GRABBER-IN-CHIEF of this great nation, has shamed, slandered, and abused women, yet many voters just look away. Why? Does anyone defend Biff Tannen when he mocks Lorraine, sexually assaults her, or shoves her to the floor? No. Why should "Biff" Trump get a pass?

How are people who ignore the bad behavior of "Biff" Trump able to do the right thing in other situations? When presented evidence of a priest's misconduct, they don't say "Yes, he abused children but he gives a great homily, so let's keep him on." Apparently anything "Biff" Trump does is "just his personal business" or "water under the bridge." And besides, "he's good for the economy."

Are our pocketbooks really more important than our morality? What does that say about us as a nation? Men, what does it say about us as men if we are able to silently overlook or excuse abusive behavior toward women?

It's impossible to overlook Biff Tannen's behavior. Throughout the *Back to the Future* trilogy, Biff doesn't ask, he simply takes what he wants, from both men and women. His perverse masculinity

29

confuses force with strength; he views women not as individuals, but as things to be taken, things that exist to serve his needs. It helps that both Biffs are over 6 feet tall. If either was a foot shorter, there's no way they would get away with acting this way. At least not in public.

In BTTF1, young Biff Tannen personifies the worst fears of American parents who send their daughters off to school each morning. Oversized and oversexed, Biff is feared by classmates and cheered on by his sidekicks, all three of whom are yes-men, fixers, and hooligans.

Biff considers himself a "dreamboat," but to a girl in his crosshairs, he's a nightmare. In the scene set in the 1955 school cafeteria, Lorraine sits at a table with a friend and Biff pulls his chair directly behind hers, preventing her escape. Though he's seated, he's terrifying in action; he's easily twice her size. He practically engulfs her; his arms snake around her as he pulls at her clothes. Back in the real world, female airline passengers have complained that "Biff" Trump's hands were all over them, too.

But 17-year-old Lorraine sticks up for herself and tells Biff to leave her alone, even as his sidekicks encourage him from the next table. The word "no" isn't in Biff's vocabulary, though, and he declares with a sneer, "You want it, you know you want it, and you know you want me to give it to you."

Later in the movie at the dance, things get even worse when Lorraine disagrees and slaps Biff. He grabs her arm and pins her in place with a look that's as fierce as his grip – and releases her only when Marty McFly rushes over and yanks him off.

It's an ugly scene, made even uglier by the fact that it takes place in full view of others. If you asked the older, successful version of Biff in BTTF2 to look back and recall his interaction with Lorraine the night he sexually assaulted her, perhaps you can imagine the casino owner describing it like this:

> *You know, I'm automatically attracted to beautiful – I just start kissing them. It's like a magnet. Just kiss. I don't even wait. And when you're a star, they let you do it. You can do anything ... grab them by the pussy. You can do anything.*[25]

These, of course, are Donald "Biff" Trump's words on the 2005 "Access Hollywood" tape.

Thirty years later as either middle-manager Biff or car-detailer Biff, does he remember this misbehavior from his school days? If thirty years later the FBI went back and interviewed the other kids in that school cafeteria or at that dance, would they remember those events the way Lorraine does? For George, his memory of the parking lot incident would be as much about punching Biff as it was about Biff's actions in the car.

But in the movie, the cameras were there and so were we. We saw it. We know what happened, just as Lorraine knows and will never forget, and we can rewind the movie and watch it again. If we don't, our memory of it will fade because we were only spectators. Lorraine was the object of the abuse and her memory won't fade – even if others doubt her.

Fast forward from 1955 to the alternate 1985 timeline in BTTF2, when Biff is a wealthy and powerful casino owner. According to Team Biff, he's now a giant among men:

> *His power and influence made him the model*
> *of world leaders and heads of state. Marvel*
> *at Biff's ongoing relationships with the rich*
> *and famous. We've all heard the legend.*
> *But who is the man?*

That's what we must ask ourselves today. Too bad it wasn't Biff Tannen who had the following conversation on a radio show, because it would be far easier to excuse these words coming from the mouth of a fictional villain than from the future president of the United States.

> *Howard Stern: Will Dakota Fanning grow up hot?*
> *Donald Trump: No. No.*
> *Stern: She will not?*
> *Trump: She will always be cute.*
> *Stern: But she'll never be hot.*
> *Trump: She'll never be hot.*[26]

Dakota Fanning was 11 years old at the time.

Trump sexualizing young girls is not a one-time incident – in a 1992 TV special, he speaks with a 14-year-old girl as she's riding up an escalator, and he says, "I am going to be dating her in ten years. Can you believe it?"[27]

"Biff" Trump's sexual thoughts roll around like a loose cannon on deck. A *very* loose cannon. When his own daughter Tiffany was an infant – just a year old – he commented and gestured on camera about what her breasts might one day look like.[28]

Many adults feel the need to give back to their communities through their PTA, Little League, or Girl Scouts. Not "Biff" Trump; the owner of the Miss Universe beauty pageant was too busy prowling around the dressing rooms of teenage contestants.

"You know, they're standing there with no clothes," said Trump, according to *Rolling Stone*.[29] "And you see these incredible-looking women. And so I sort of get away with things like that." These young women later recalled feeling like "cattle" being graded by the rancher who owned them.

Now let's compare the two men's current marriages. Both Biff and "Biff" show a repeated and willful lack of concern about their wives, as if they were chattel, or even just cattle.

Lorraine Tannen is Biff's abused, unloved third wife. Their relationship is usurious. If we look back at the video clip of the day they got married, we hear Biff saying "Number three's a charm" as he pushes his tongue into Lorraine's mouth, ignoring her discomfort and disgust. This, on their wedding day.

"Biff" Trump's third wife, Melania, has recently displayed frostiness toward him in public, including incidents when she wouldn't hold his hand. Numerous times she's decided not to appear in public with her husband, or even travel in the same vehicle with him. It must be difficult for her today to hear explicit details of his times with Stormy Daniels and Karen McDougal – from a time when Barron was just an infant.

In BTTF3, Biff Tannen lounges in a jacuzzi with two women while his wife is in the building; Lorraine could have walked in on them just as easily as her son Marty does. "Biff" Trump gave Playboy Playmate Karen McDougal a tour of his New York apartment shortly after Melania had given birth to their son, Barron. Assured that Melania wasn't in the building, Ms. McDougal asked about the staff. "Biff" told her "they won't say anything" – as if they knew the drill, they knew the score.[30]

Multiple wives and women, accusations of multiple offenses and denials from Trump, but sexual perpetrators almost always deny their guilt.

"You could have just walked away."

These are Seamus McFly's words of wisdom to his great-grandson Marty in BTTF3 after Biff goads Marty. This was meant to teach Marty that masculinity doesn't require responding to violence with violence, to reassure him that no one would think less of him if he'd simply walked away.

But what about people who sometimes *can't* walk away? Like your daughter, your mother or sister.

"Biff" Trump is in a position of dominance when he meets his prey; he's the boss, a rich man, TV star, beauty pageant owner, or even president. Walking away simply isn't a choice for many women. And what about the countless others who *did* walk away, those who *did* have a choice? How many are out there and have yet to speak up?

Ask "Biff" about his attitude toward women and he'll tell you he was one of the first to promote women to high positions in a male-dominated field. This is somewhat true – but remember, when he promoted them, he was in charge, he was in control.

But when he's confronted with a woman who's his equal, not an underling, Trump displays ape-like dominance and an imagined superiority. When meeting with Angela Merkel, the Chancellor of Germany and one of the most powerful women in the world, "Biff" Trump refused to shake her hand. On another occasion, he flung candy[31] on a table in front of her, saying "don't say I never give you anything."[32] Trump referred to the Prime Minister of the U.K. by her first name, Theresa, instead of her title; he didn't bow to Queen Elizabeth and later walked in front of her because he couldn't be bothered to learn protocol.

And his stalky, leering performance during the second presidential debate[33] with Hillary Clinton raised the hackles of many women watching.

Whether interacting with women in power or with more vulnerable women, "Biff" Trump reveals his utter lack of respect. He objectifies women; they're merely things for him to use. More than a dozen accusations of sexual assault have been lodged against him.

Biff Tannen and "Biff" Trump are the same man. No introspection, no regret about their infidelities, no compassion, no sympathy for their partners. Serve the self, do it *right now*, and move on.

There is no chance the original Biff will ever address these issues, but in the real world, "Biff" Trump should. Brett Kavanaugh's anger before the Senate Judiciary Committee in September 2018 and Trump's demeaning responses to the accusations leveled at him over the years show how hard it is to effect societal change on this topic. Nearly 20 percent of American women have experienced rape or attempted rape during their lifetimes,[34] often committed by someone they know,[35] but false accusations are very rare.[36] A man has no clue how the possibility of sexual assault can shape a woman's behavior at a social gathering or when considering the safety of transportation options or public restrooms – or even walking down the street.

For the good of all American people, Trump (and Kavanaugh) must exhume and prioritize these issues, not deny and bury them.

Women exist only to serve men's primal needs, after all. Biff and "Biff" both are devoid of morals and unbound by cultural norms. When it comes to interacting with women, they either don't know or don't give a damn what kind of behavior is acceptable – or even legal.

CHAPTER 11 ⫸ LOSER!

"Now that you are about to play my game, I invite you to live the fantasy! Feel the power! And make the deals!"
~ *TRUMP The Game*, discontinued by manufacturer

L ET'S START BY NOTING THIS BALD FACT: Trump's companies have filed for Chapter 11 bankruptcy protection six times.[37] Each time, Trump has smartly shed boatloads of debt. "Biff" Trump calls it smart, and "using certain laws that are there," but that's probably not the way his lenders saw it as they watched "Biff" walk off with hundreds of millions of their money. Imagine how it would feel if you took out a mortgage on your house, and lent "Biff" Trump that money. He then blew through it, declared bankruptcy, and flew off in his private jet, leaving you with a worthless piece of paper.

But is Biff Tannen a good businessman? Let's consider his various business roles over time.

In 1955, he's the school bully who intimidates the hapless George McFly. His "business" then is to get George to do his homework, which he does. Fast-forward to 1985 and Biff is a mid-level manager – 30 years older, and still a bully. He doesn't seem that bright, and he continues to force George to do his work and stamps his own name on the product.

When George delivers a single, humiliating, knockout punch to stop Biff from raping Lorraine, it changes the future and Biff's place in it: at the movie's conclusion, Biff is no longer a manager, but a car detailer at George's beck and call. Even with the tables turned, Biff remains Biff: a low-wattage slacker, a con and a character who's "always trying to get away with something."

Then in BTTF2 when the sequel shifts to an alternate 1985, we see that things have changed "bigly" for Biff. He's become a man with tremendous wealth, power, and political clout. A man sprung from humble beginnings who with a bit of "luck" built an empire from toxic waste and now owns a casino-hotel business, his crown jewel.

But sometimes the fake gems shine the brightest. A single event changed everything – Biff got hold of *Gray's Sports Almanac*. He simply got lucky. Donald "Biff" Trump got lucky too, born a member of the Lucky Sperm Club thanks to his father's success as a real estate developer. A million-dollar loan from Dad launched Donnie's career, and he followed in his father's footsteps into the property development business. Without that start, "Biff" Trump might still be a mid-level manager or washing cars.

Also-ran ... A casino

In the casino business, the house always wins – eventually. Whether a casino can take in money quickly enough to pay its bills and debts becomes the question that determines financial success or failure, separating winning casinos from the losers.

In BTTF2, Biff seems to be a winner. Though still a noxious, aggressive bully, he's a successful (if immoral) one.

But Donald Trump is a loser. Despite his claims (all talk and no cattle), "Biff" Trump simply isn't a smart operator when he ventures away from his father's original business: the real estate industry. Even there, his best deals – the deals that required complex negotiations – were in his earliest work completed over three decades ago, and he never came close to the dizzying heights reached by other property developers in New York.[38]

In the casino business, too, "Biff" Trump was a loser. Compared with true industry heavyweights such as Sheldon Adelson, Steve Wynn, or Stanley Ho, Trump was never more than a small fish in a big pond – a mere minnow, really. And not just a minnow, but a bankrupt minnow. Between 1991 and 2014, Trump Hotels and Casinos Resorts filed for Chapter 11 bankruptcy not once, but four times.

Donald "Biff" Trump is certainly not "the greatest dealmaker in the history of our country."[39] Most of his revenue now comes from licensing his name to other businesses, and its value will vary considerably depending on his popularity as president. So far, it's not going too well.

Ironically, in his negotiations with his ghostwriter for royalties over *The Art of the Deal*, Trump reveals just how inept he can be as a dealmaker. Not only did the writer get half the book's advance and royalties, he also earned equal billing on the cover, with his name the same size as Trump's. When asked by a reporter how he haggled such a great deal, the author replied that "Biff" Trump "basically just agreed."[40]

The list of Trump's outright business failures is well known, including Trump Airlines, Trump Magazine, Trump Steaks, Trump Vodka, Trump: The Game, and Trump University – which not only failed, but was also the subject of multiple class-action and state lawsuits for fraud.

His hotel business? Well, it's smaller than you might believe and dwarfed by bigger competitors such as Marriott, Sheraton, or Hilton. Though the Trump Organization has about 22,000 employees, Starbucks is ten times that size, Intercontinental Hotels fifteen times larger; Walmart, the largest private employer in the U.S., is a whopping 100 times larger.

And size does matter – at least in business. It really, really matters to "Biff" Trump because he claims his business experience is the reason he's singularly qualified to lead a country that directly employs 2.7 million people.

Trump is *such* a bad businessman that he would be worth more today if he had stopped working in 1978 and simply invested his money in an index fund, a type of mutual fund with relatively low risk/reward.[41] Sad!

The myth of Trump as a savvy dealmaker was created by his greatest triumph: an acting job. On *The Apprentice* TV series, for its first 14 seasons, Donald "Biff" Trump acted (or impersonated) the role of a successful businessman so convincingly that people now believe that's who he is. But it was an acting gig! George Clooney isn't a surgeon because he portrayed one on *ER* and playing an oil tycoon on *Dallas* didn't make Larry Hagman one in real life. Trump simply is not the character that he played on TV.

Now "Biff" Trump is playacting the role of president of the USA – but without preparation and practice he's failing desperately. Sad, because he's out of his depth and ad-libbing – really, really badly. In the private sector, in the real corporate world, a free-wheeling "listen-to-my-gut" business person might hurt a company's prospects or leave investors lighter in the pockets. But there's much more at stake here. Says Deepak Malhotra, a professor of negotiation at Harvard Business School, "When you behave this way in the public sector ... other people get hurt."[42]

※

Would you want Biff Tannen from BTTF2 as your president? Take a hard look at ~~Hill~~ Hell Valley where Biff reigns as one of America's richest and most powerful men. Look out through the doors of his plush casino at the anarchy outside. Gangs of bikers and criminals fill the town square; an armored tank patrols it. Smoke and soot billow from factories, while local commerce is limited to peep shows and sex services, bail bondsmen, and pawnshops – places that tend to cater to the human misery caused by gambling.

Consider, too, the people that Biff Tannen surrounds himself with. The three flunkies who helped him terrorize other students back in high school are still around 30 years later. The goons, now grown up, have little going for them other than their allegiance to Biff and a willingness to enforce his whims. They're hardly the town's best and brightest – presumably Biff, like "Biff" Trump, doesn't want anyone in his circle who might ever challenge him or become a real threat. Biff Tannen chooses loyal puppets just as Trump does. President "Biff" will always hire a compliant underling over a competent one. He doesn't want pushback or reason: He wants people to do his bidding while pretending they're not.

But more important, why would anyone want a businessperson as president? What is so appealing about that notion? Though a CEO possesses qualities that may seem advantageous – like competitiveness or efficiency – they are offset by traits that could be harmful.

For example, most corporate leaders focus on deliberately narrow goals; they aim to maximize profits and are rewarded financially for doing so. They often have little or no regard for other consumers who do not, could not, or would not purchase their products, because those people will never affect profit. It's simple.

They don't think or care about "externalities" like how their products might affect the environment or society – as long as their businesses comply with the law. A fast food manufacturer can make the country obese without bearing the costs of lower productivity and medical expenses. An oil company can pump oil from the ground and turn it into exhaust fumes and CO_2 without repairing the damage it causes. At their worst, corporations and the people charged with leading them are exploiters that legally profit from scarce resources, a lack of competition, or false advertising.

Biff Tannen is unconcerned by the dystopia outside his hotel – hell, he's probably profiting from it all. Surrounded by the trappings of his wealth, he doesn't care about the social impacts of his toxic waste and gambling ventures.

He's a successful businessman, but would he make a good president of the United States? Likely not. Even great business people may not make good presidents. The jobs are completely different, require completely different skill sets, and their success is determined by completely different outcomes.

The president of the United States must serve all its citizens: the rich and the poor, the greedy and the needy, the fans who voted yes and the voters who said no. The federal government directly employs 2.7 million people, and it is the job of the president to direct them while reconciling the diverse opinions of many special-interest groups. This is not the job of a businessman.

With few exceptions, the president cannot dictate. Instead, the politician must cajole and shepherd and bark and compromise while working with the democratically elected Congress, other nations, global organizations, and myriad other groups and individuals to create and enact and monitor policy, to inspire, and to lead the nation forward. Is this Biff Tannen? No. Does this describe President "Biff" Trump? Certainly not.

In the first *Back to the Future* movie, Doc Brown in 1955 taunts Marty with, "Tell me, future boy, who's president of the United States in 1985?" At least in Ronald Reagan, America got an actor who had the experience to succeed in the role; he was president of the Screen Actors Guild for seven years and then governor of California for two terms before he was president.

Today, we have President "Biff" Trump: a failing businessman-turned-TV-actor who has brought Biff's taste and sensibilities to the White House, along with his bullying ways. Do we see him passing small-business-friendly policies and improving the well-being of the man on the street? No, we see big businesses protected at the expense of consumers. Just like the "house always wins" approach in casinos, decisions by Biff and "Biff" always favor themselves and their cronies. They fill their own pockets and leave the gamblers to return home after blowing their kids' education fund at the craps table, and leave the voters to wake up and find their consumer protections, environmental protections, and the social safety net gone.

For a window into "Biff" Trump's soul, just look beyond his gluttony. Look past the ornate homes, the oversized and gaudy furnishings, the towering skyscrapers and prime real estate, the many grand entrances. Beyond the showy glamor, there's simply nothing there! It's nothing more than stage management with a heavy layer of gilt and hours on the tanning bed.

"Biff" Trump revels in the comparisons to P.T. Barnum, the showman known for the line "There's a sucker born every minute." But who's the sucker here?

SAD! Donald 'Biff' Trump Is President

SMALL TOWN USA

Well I was born in a small town, and I live in a small town
Probably die in a small town, oh those small communities
~ John Cougar Mellencamp

B IFF TANNEN WAS BORN IN HILL VALLEY and stayed there. Donald "Biff" Trump was born in New York City and stayed *there*. So how did Donald "Biff" Trump – a man of the metropolis, gold leaf, and trust funds – manage to pitch, win, and hold Small Town USA?

How did Trump nudge Kenosha County, Wisconsin (population 168,065), Monroe County, Michigan (population 152,021) and Erie County, Pennsylvania (population 280,566) all into the Republican column? These are towns and cities he knew nothing of, towns he had no understanding of nor empathy for. It was just 107,000 votes in those three states that swung the 2016 presidential election to "Biff" Trump.

"Biff" did it because he's a great pitch man. On the stump, he knows how to rile up a crowd without logic or facts. He cooks up a thick stew of nostalgia steeped in fear and then sprinkles salt and salaciousness on top. The smalltown voters sip it, smile, and sup. "Biff" sells "let's get back to the good ol' days," where everyone had a job, workers stood in front of machines making things, and miners dug up coal; back when the mighty white majority was all they knew.

In 2016 he basically was selling snake oil. Donald "Biff" Trump knew nothing of those days, those communities, or their people. But they clung to him as a savior offering a miracle balm; he knew the balm wouldn't work, but that didn't matter, because before everyone found him out, he'd be in the Oval Office selling new nonsense.

✳

A place can't be both a hill and a valley, so BTTF's "Hill Valley" serves as a metaphor for a place that exists in the collective imagination: a safe, clean, spiffy place with a malt shop and a full-service gas station. Indeed, Marty repeats the word "dream" three times when he gets there.

Hill Valley is the kind of place you find in the Republican heartland between the liberal coasts, home to voters who elected "Biff" Trump in 2016 and who still support him today. We know that Hill Valley in the movie is set in California, and might have been based on Grass Valley or a similar town somewhere near it. Grass Valley is a town of about 13,000 people just under 60 miles from Sacramento and about 90 miles from Reno. Today its rich gold mines are long gone, but it has a diverse economy including tourism, agriculture, wineries, and technology.

In Hill Valley 1955, we see no hint of the national unrest that was simmering across the country at the time. Women, many of whom had taken on traditional male roles during WWII, had set aside their Rosie the Riveter uniforms and more or less happily settled back into homemaking. In Montgomery, Alabama in 1955, Rosa Parks refused to give up her seat on a public bus. And though the Korean War had ended in 1953 and the U.S. was already actively involved in Vietnam, you don't see any of that in the movie – or from draft-dodging "Biff" Trump either.

In Hill Valley in 1955, the downtown is vibrant. The historic courthouse and clock tower sit in a grassy town square ringed by family-owned businesses. The center of the town is friendly and walkable, and the streets buzz with nice pedestrian traffic. The few cars – all American-made, of course, no foreign models – are fueled up at a full-service gas station, and the McFly family home is on a leafy street in a nice neighborhood.

Hill Valley 1955 lives up to its welcome sign, which proclaims it "a nice place to live." The many logos on the welcome sign show how important community is in Hill Valley; they advertise an active Chamber of Commerce, YMCA, United States Junior Chamber, Camp Fire, American Legion Auxiliary, the National Grange of the Order of Patrons of Husbandry, Optimist International, and Future Farmers of America.

In a rural area just outside Hill Valley, we see Lyon Estates, a real-estate development where ground has just been broken. It's the suburb where the McFly family will live in 1985, and it is representative of the 11 million suburban homes that were built in the U.S. between 1948 and 1958, changing how and where much of America would live.[43]

Now fast-forward to Hill Valley 1985, which we see in two scenarios based on whether or not Biff Tannen (or by proxy "Biff" Trump) takes control of the town. In BTTF1 when bully Biff ends up as a car detailer, Hill Valley is a bit run down. With suburban spread, the town square has changed; 1955's Hill Valley Stationers, Lou's Café, and Elite Barber Shop by 1985 have become Cupid's Adult Books, Lou's Aerobic Fitness Center, and an empty store with a "moved to Twin Pines Mall" sign.

In BTTF2, in the alternate 1985 Hill Valley (or Hell Valley) where Biff is in power, those three stores have alternately become Hell Hole, War Zone, and Bangkok Sauna and Asian Massage. This is libertarianism and capitalism gone mad. The town is barely recognizable; its good "Midwestern" values have been sold down the river by the short-term promises of a single man. A con man. Biff.

After polluting Hill Valley with his toxic waste reclamation plants, Biff in 1979 successfully lobbied to legalize gambling and then converted the historic Hill Valley Courthouse into a casino/hotel, Biff Tannen's Pleasure Palace. (Echoes here of "Biff"

Trump's conversion of the Old Post Office at 1100 Pennsylvania Avenue into a D.C. luxury hotel.)

Biff Tannen's empire has spread further into real estate in alt-1985. The entry gate to Lyon Estates, where Marty's family home used to be, now bears a sign stating that the subdivision is a "Proud Member of the BiffCo Family" – under heavy graffiti. Gangs drive down streets in the evening raking the properties with gunfire. Many of the houses have BiffCo "For Sale" signs posted in the front yards.

Biff doesn't seem to care. He's rich, he's got his big name on his big casino, and there's even a museum dedicated to the myth of manhood. Biff doesn't care about the misery and crime that result from his businesses. For him, it's all about profits and ego and sex, nothing else.

※

Hill Valley alt-1985 looks a lot like Atlantic City, New Jersey, during its darkest days when "Biff" Trump took over and promised greatness. It wasn't to be. Atlantic City, though sorry to see him go, was in the same sorry state as it was before he came. Gambling didn't solve its problems. "Hell" Valley in 1985, as graffiti on the welcome sign illustrates, has become a study of haves and have-nots, when property and power are in the hands of the 1 percent, or worse, one single man.

What is clear in the BTTF trilogy: the effects of long-running cultural and economic trends that have left a mark on the American landscape. The BTTF films have been named the most important movie about urbanism because as the characters travel through time, we watch Hill Valley as it undergoes the same fate as many small towns in America after a national housing boom shifted life to the suburbs.[44]

"Biff" Trump's pitch about mining and "making stuff" is just twaddle. This won't save those little towns. Talk like this will only retard their rejuvenation. Rather than propping up zombie industries, it's better to just rip off the Band-Aid and use subsidies and grants to transform the communities now, once and for all, and save them from their inexorable slide into decrepitude and poverty. But "Biff" Trump is pandering, plain and simple, talking economic nonsense and showering Small Town USA with false hope. He's stealing money from their children's futures while keeping the parents hooked on the crack-high of believing there's still life in those good ol' ways.

Imagine the absurdity of Hill Valley in 1985 deciding to reopen the 1885 Delgado Mine, shown in BTTF3. Imagine how much federal money would be wasted to get it functioning again, to get it back to a break-even point where it's creating new jobs. Even then, would Hill Valley's citizens actually want to go down a mine shaft to work in the dark each and every day? Trump would see the mine differently: He would consider it a natural resource to be extracted and exploited for profit, regardless of the environmental or global consequences. He would probably pitch the redevelopment of the Delgado Mine much as he did recently in his muddled and incoherent speech to the good Republicans of Utica, New York.

"... if they would have allowed a little bit of fracking and taken some of the richness out of the land ... because stuff flows ... and all of a sudden someday you're not going to have that underground maybe so much. "[45]

These are the words of an incoherent moron.

✳

Like it or not, the non-Caucasian population of America is growing rapidly while the Caucasian population is growing much more slowly. This can't be reversed no matter what "Biff" Trump says and no matter what laws he passes and no matter how many children he "detains" in "camps" around the country. What we as a nation must do is to differentiate between the hard-working, productive, and positive people and the lazy, unproductive, and negative people. *That should be the dividing line* where we cast judgment, not based on skin color, sex, religion, dress, or nationality.

The "Biff" in the White House doesn't like these changes and he wants to describe the transition as scary and dangerous. He pitches patriotism – even at the U.N. gathering – yet this talk of patriotism is coming from a draft-dodger who didn't want to fight because of "bone spurs" and doesn't pay taxes because of tricky accounting maneuvers. "Biff" Trump the patriot, Trump the taxpayer, Trump the protector of smalltown America? It's a joke. He's a capitalist exploiter. He's an orange-skinned chameleon who slides and glides around tongue-flickering, saying whatever comes to mind as necessary to advance his own agenda.

Look instead to Mike Pence to see a true Midwesterner. No one can argue that he is not the real deal. He's a native of Indiana, he gets what a hog roast is, he understands the importance of Little League and church on Sunday. He knows that a community is a web of ties to those around you. He's "Midwestern nice," straightforward, not prone to throwing his toys out of the playpen. Look at Pence. You may not like him, especially if you are left-leaning, but he is authentic.

"Biff" Trump pitched a return to the America once cherished, to a place where small towns prospered, communities were tight-knit, Midwestern family values still meant something, and – above all else – America was Number One. But "Biff" never lived in nor even liked small towns; his community is Mar-a-Lago, with his 62,500-square-foot house and his billionaire neighbors; his family includes children from three wives, each progressively younger. "Biff" Trump hates unions. He hates worker power. He hates taxes.

Even his slogan, "Make America Great Again," was borrowed. Ronald Reagan used this when he was the Republican nominee for president in 1980.

Working people: This is your guy?

Citizens of Kenosha, Utica, Erie, and Monroe; of Wisconsin, New York, Pennsylvania, and Michigan: Look at the "alt" Hill Valley in BTTF2 and see your future in an unregulated world dedicated solely to the pursuit of capitalism.

If you choose to ignore the environmental impacts of fracking, drilling, and climate change, or manage to overlook the social costs of income inequality, you allow American civility and decency to fray – and you too will have a casino and porn shops; you too will have armored vehicles in your town squares; and you too will wake up in Hell Valley.

SAD! Donald 'Biff' Trump Is President

UNRAVELING THE SPACE-TIME CONTINUUM

Tell me, doctor, where are we going this time
Is this the '50s or 1999
Gotta get back in time, gotta get back in time.
~ Huey Lewis and the News (1985)

COULD "BIFF" TRUMP, WHO'S SO SIMILAR to Biff Tannen, have traveled back in time to gain the advantage he needed to win the 2016 election? After all, for what purpose did old Biff go back from 2015 to 1955 but for the almighty dollar?

Through time travel, characters in the *Back to the Future* trilogy are able to rewrite or restore the future depending on where they go and when they go there. So, for example, Marty ensures his parents fall in love in BTTF1, saves his future children from a life of crime in BTTF2, and prevents Doc's murder in BTTF3.

And old Biff in BTTF2 transports the stolen *Sports Almanac* to his younger self in 1955 so he can use its knowledge to become rich and powerful. He could have looked deeper into himself and sought to figure out why he was a bully, chosen a completely new direction, and made a change to become a better person. He could have thought about his family or about the reasons he still lived with his grandmother, or could have gone back even further to fix his parents' lives, like Marty did.

But no, the streak of selfishness was always there. Old Biff doesn't try to change young Biff's personality because he knows the leopard would not – could not – change his spots. Goodness goes against the grain for Biff who, like a wild animal, is driven by base instinct.

So he just handed himself the *Sports Almanac*, and with it, the golden ticket.

"Biff" Trump would likely take a trip in the DeLorean out of similar instincts: for vengeance, to settle an old score, for profit, maybe to switch one wife out for another, or to tip an election in his favor. We'll never know, but he likely wouldn't be curing cancer or donating money to charity.

Looking back over Trump's campaign for the Republican candidacy – and later, the presidency – it's still shocking how unconventional they were and how "Biff" Trump seemed to snatch victory from the jaws of defeat. Did he have a DeLorean? Did he use it to tweak his performance and win after-the-fact? Perhaps you and I unknowingly lived through that time while "Biff" Trump went back in time over and over again, creating little time tangents until he finally got it right and managed to win the election against all odds.

Let's return to the evening of August 6, 2015, the night when Fox News hosted the first Republican debate. There are 10 candidates on stage and news anchor Megyn Kelly, one of the moderators, poses this question to Trump:

KELLY: "Mr. Trump, one of the things people love about you is you speak your mind and you don't use a politician's filter. However, that is not without its downsides, in particular when it comes to women. You've called women you don't like fat pigs, dogs, slobs, and disgusting animals. Your Twitter account ..."

TRUMP (interrupting): "Only Rosie O'Donnell."[46]

[RESOUNDING AUDIENCE APPLAUSE/CHEERING]

But as the camera then pans over the debate audience, we see that it's divided. Many people are smiling or laughing, even clapping. Others sit stone-faced and motionless.

Why did half the audience, including both men and women, respond so positively to Trump's cruel taunt? Could Trump – using the DeLorean – have taken the opportunity to test different responses and found the one that worked the best? Or was it the sheer shock factor of the inappropriate insult that startled the audience into laughter? Whatever it was, "Biff" Trump never looked back and never pulled his punches – nor was he ever held accountable for what he said.

Of course, it's also possible that someone else futzed around with the space-time continuum. Maybe Vladimir Putin, exasperated by Hillary Clinton, sent a small Russian interference team through time to manipulate the 2016 election.

Then again, it could simply be that the audience actually wanted a boxing match, preferring jabs, hooks, and knockout blows to a political debate. Let's hope not. That would a harbinger for the end of intelligent debate, and political campaigns would be just part of primetime TV entertainment.

And what if we had the chance to borrow the DeLorean and go back in time ourselves? Where or when exactly would we go? As we learned from Doc Brown, time travel is tricky. You have to be v-e-r-y careful what you tinker with, or you could "create a time paradox ... that would unravel the very fabric of the space-time continuum and destroy the entire universe."

That means we can't go too far back in time or choose a moment that involves too many people, for fear of doing something that wipes out the historical record. So we can't kidnap Donald and we shouldn't waste time on getting Stormy Daniels' story out in the final few weeks: that might or might not change anything.

To stop Biff's rise to power in BTTF2, Doc and Marty had to pinpoint the exact moment when Biff first got hold of *Gray's Sports Almanac*. Then they hopped into the DeLorean, traveled back in time, and tweaked the past just enough to destroy the *Sports Almanac*. In doing so, they created a new time tangent, but one in which the future is better for everyone in Hill Valley – except Biff. We should try to do the same.

.

BARACK, DO NOT PISS TRUMP OFF!

This was all your fault, Barack Obama.

H E SET THE BALL ROLLING, AFTER ALL, on April 26, 2011 when he tore into "Biff" Trump at the White House Correspondents' Dinner:

> ... all kidding aside, obviously, we all know about your credentials and breadth of experience. For example – no, seriously, just recently, in an episode of Celebrity Apprentice at the steakhouse, the men's cooking team did not impress the judges from Omaha Steaks. And there was a lot of blame to go around. But you, Mr. Trump, recognized that the real problem was a lack of leadership. And so ultimately, you didn't blame Lil' Jon or Meatloaf. You fired Gary Busey. And these are the kind of decisions that would keep me up at night. Well handled, sir. Well handled.[47]

Thin-skinned "Biff" Trump seethed silently during that speech, humiliated live in front of the hundreds of journalists and celebrities in the room and the thousands of people who later watched online as President Obama taunted him. This could have been the very moment that Trump decided "I'm going to show them," and years later his humiliation resulted in his running in and winning the 2016 election.

If we traveled back to that moment, the favor we'd ask of Obama would be simple: "Please change your speech; just pick on someone else." Obama's lobbed jokes would have rolled off a more confident man. But they sliced through Trump's paper-thin skin and enraged him so much that years later, he's spending significant effort and time repealing Obama's legacy, piece-by-piece and point-by-point, to pay him back.

Second choices

If we could get to him in the past, Obama, a highly intelligent and considerate leader, would probably listen. We could suggest that he appoint "Biff" Trump to a government position. In 2015, Penny Pritzker was Secretary of Commerce, but Obama would have been loath to swap her out for "Biff" because "Biff" is simply not smart enough and wouldn't toe the line – or read his papers or really do anything cohesive.

Obama could have named Trump a goodwill ambassador of sorts. The position and exact role wouldn't have mattered much, as long as it was very much in the public eye and depended on a grasp of certain technical knowledge. We know that Trump would not have been able to master the details, which would likely have generated all kinds of random blowback ("You're fired!") and prevented him from seriously considering a political future.

We could go back much further and find a felony to prosecute Trump for, which, if on his record, would disqualify him for running for president. It might also be fun to prod James Comey to start the FBI's investigation of Trump University earlier, although Trump did shrug off a lot of real and "fake" baggage during his campaign. We could try to talk to Megyn Kelly before the debate, but our intervention would be such a juicy story itself that she would likely pivot and make our intervention the headline news.

In trying to change the past, we would likely experience as many time paradoxes as we do when watching the *Back to the Future* movies. If there were no President Trump – if Hillary Clinton or any other candidate had become president – there would have been no Sean Spicer nor Sarah Huckabee Sanders on the daily news, no White House Chief of Staff Reince Priebus, no Scaramucci, no National Security Adviser Mike Flynn.

And it's a good bet that "Biff" Trump would have been just as happy *not* being president and not being ridiculed every day. At the end of each of the *BTTF* movies, Biff Tannen doesn't look any happier no matter whether he's a car detailer, a casino magnate, or an outlaw.

We can wish about the future, we can wonder about the past, and we can work through all kinds of what-ifs, but all we really have is *now*. Time travel is, as yet, impossible, but our future hasn't been written yet. We're writing it as we go along, and the only way to correct the past and improve tomorrow is to make good decisions right now.

MAKE AMERICA GREAT AGAIN!

Let's Get Back to the Future

*M*ANY TV VIEWERS ARE NOT FANS of professional wrestling, because – for one reason – it's unclear where the action ends and the acting starts. It is not "real" wrestling, but it's not very good acting either. The wrestlers sometimes get hurt, but more often these performers are just pretending.

No one in this country imagined that an angry foul-mouthed overweight 70-year-old rich man in a red hat could step into the ring, defeat all comers, and become president of the United States.

Imagine that Biff Tannen was elected class president of Hill Valley High School in 1955. That could have gone two ways: He might have turned a moral corner, realized his responsibility to others and grown up, or he could have dumbed-down and doubled-down even further to use his position to harass and molest Lorraine. Which way do you think Biff would have chosen?

Now imagine that the crooked, casino-owning Biff Tannen in BTTF2 was elected president of the United States in 1985. He had already destroyed the community of "Hell" Valley and built a great business out of vice. He had put violence on the streets. Do we see any hint in that movie of his caring for anyone other than himself? His "care" for his (third) wife is evident as he shoves her to the floor, and for his children as he gut-punches Marty. All he seems to care about is sex and money.

Just himself. That's his focus and his field view.

When we consider the movies – fiction, of course – we all agree that Biff should not be class president and certainly not president of the United States. Now step back out of the movie and ask why we elected "Biff" Trump as president in 2016 when he was (and still is) so Tannen-esque? Why did we do that?

As the headlines parade past us, remember that our actions matter. Even little actions. Marty's brave dash to push George out of the way of an oncoming car had profound ripple effects throughout BTTF1. Young Biff's receipt of the *Sports Almanac* from old Biff changed the world of BTTF2. Sometimes the flap of butterfly wings in Brazil can cause a tornado in Texas. Stay alert and take action – even small actions. Don't give up, because the consequences of that could be just ...

Biffhorrific.

That's actually the nickname of BTTF2's alternate 1985 timeline when Biff Tannen, sleazy casino magnate, sold the citizens of Hill Valley down the river with the promise of industry and jobs, while sacrificing the long-term prosperity of the community to pad his own pockets.

You do not want to see Tannen in power and we do not want "Biff" Trump to turn New York into a twisted version of "Survivor: America."

With no curbs on power, this complex and beautiful country would be little more than a reality show, but with far graver consequences. In Hill Valley 1955, Principal Strickland keeps Biff in check. Sure, he picks on Marty, but he also disciplines Biff Tannen (who reluctantly complies). Strickland does the same in 1885, when as marshal of Hill Valley, he checks the worst instincts of "Mad Dog" Tannen.

✳

But who is the marshal in America in 2018?

"Biff" is now president of the United States. Who will curb his excesses to thwart his misguided impulses?[48] Maybe Congress? Obviously not. His advisors? No – he chews them up and spits them out like gum. Only life-long Republican Robert Mueller stands as possible check today. He wears the marshal's badge for now.

But note: in BTTF3 the marshal survives; a death scene was filmed, but it was later deleted because it was too sad to include.[49] In it, Biff confronts Marshal Strickland outside of town. After they agree to let each other pass, "Mad Dog" Tannen shoots Strickland in the back, killing him right in front of his young son. Don't let "Mad Dog" Trump shoot you in the back.

Press poison

We see the world before and after Biff's rise on the front pages of the *Hill Valley Telegraph* and *USA Today* (Hill Valley Edition), and the headlines show the differences between a well-governed society and one run by an unchecked megalomaniac.

Before Biff's rise to power, headlines in the *Hill Valley Telegraph* tell of a compromise housing bill sent for Eisenhower's okay, of the Senate extending a deadline, and stricter rules that are sought to keep parks clean.

After Biff Tannen's big winning bet in 1955 – using the stolen *Gray's Sports Almanac* – the headlines start to change:

Hike of Steel Prices Uncertain After Break

Burnett Blames JFK for Violence

Troops End Riot

And the news gets worse as Biff accumulates more power and wealth.

By 1985 he is one of the richest men in America and the headlines reflect a society that's completely broken:

Demonstrators Jailed in Clock Tower Clash

Iran Cuts Off Oil

**BiffCo to Build New Dioxin Plant;
More Jobs Will Bolster Local Economy**

Tannen Birthplace Declared National Monument

The rise of a single man shaped the public discourse of society – and that's the fear today in America.

"Biff" Trump today repeatedly calls the press "fake news" and declares the media "the enemy of the American people."[50] His attacks on the media are relentless and they threaten one of the founding principles of this country; such attacks put real lives at risk and strike fear in the hearts and minds of journalists.[51]

Online harassment (including death threats) of journalists who speak against him is now common. "Biff" Trump hasn't yet gone as far as Buford "Mad Dog" Tannen in BTTF3, who shot and killed a newspaper editor who'd printed an unfavorable story about Tannen in 1884.

However, in January 2016, Donald "Biff" Trump did say "I could stand in the middle of Fifth Avenue and shoot somebody and I wouldn't lose voters."[52]

Though he said it as a "joke," what kind of person makes a quip like that on the stump? Really, what kind of person does that?

10 billion dollars and a pardon

Our country has a chance to make a different choice in 2020. But what if we can't wait that long? Are there any other options? Sure, the 25th Amendment allows for the removal of the president from office if he's unable to discharge his duties, and Article II addresses impeachment, but neither of these will ever fly – they'll take too long and be too contentious, and Trump couldn't give a fig about the Constitution anyway.

There's a much simpler way. Deal.

He says he's a dealmaker. Okay, let's make a deal. Everything has a price for "Biff," so let's buy him out of his contract. Talk to Rudy and put a number in front of him, say five billion – cash – and start haggling. He'll get the price up to ten billion, add a pardon for himself and his family members, and heck, maybe even toss in a network TV show and we might be close.

The U.S. has a $19-trillion economy, so even small tweaks can make a big difference. Allowing a man like Trump to throw a monkey wrench in the works will mean that the economy will start to jam up; $10 billion is just a fraction of one percent of GDP. We could swallow that if we could all get back to work and sleep easy at night.

Good night and good luck

If we believe that civility, decency, and moral values are important to this country, then what the hell are we doing? We're bringing Hell Valley to Silicon Valley, Biff's three dorks to New York, swapping Bannon for Tannen, and turning Main Street into the swamp. The world is upside down and we're barely hanging on.

There is hope. You have a vote. You must use it.

Republicans, you need to think about how to get Mike Pence to the *Resolute* desk and then toss the "deranged dotard" out of the White House.[53] Democrats, don't stay home. You need to spread the word and march to the polls. Most important, we all need to start talking to each other again and remember that compromise is not just tolerable but essential.

"Biff" Trump likes to cozy up to "strong" dictators. He admires force and strength, which is exactly why he shouldn't be president. Fundamentally, in his heart, he does not believe in democracy. He does not believe in representing the people – he believes in directing people. He believes in a command economy and he is in command. Everything he does is heresy to American democracy.

You don't have to dislike "Biff" Trump. Some part of all of us laughs at the absurd, especially in the heat of the moment. You can laugh at his jokes, you can clap when he creates funny nicknames like

"Rocket Man" or "Sloppy Steve," you can even admire his aggression if you want to, but when you consider who should run this complex thing that is our country, think carefully of temperament, of even-handedness, of grace under pressure.

Instancy and theater have become more important than considered response. Platforms such as Twitter encourage the basest instincts to be shared in the shortest period of time, inciting rancor in real time, so the world can watch – and indeed join in – the vitriol and the verbal ping-pong.

If only the TV audience had booed "Biff" Trump's jibe about Rosie O'Donnell during that debate. If only they had ignored his grandstanding since then.

But that's in the past. We do have an opportunity to boo in the 2018 midterm elections and to boo again in the 2020 elections – and politicians will hear us loud and clear. We don't have a DeLorean or a *Gray's Sports Almanac* to change the future. Only a voice and a vote.

So vote.

Republicans: You have your Supreme Court. You have your tax overhaul. If "Biff" Trump is impeached, you even get President Pence.

Democrats: Don't stay home, don't give up, never accept the orange clown.

We don't want bully Biff Tannen running this country. We want "Biff" out of the White House. Tell Trump "You're fired!"

When you vote, check a different box, a better box, and let's Make America Great Again!

AFTERWORD: PRESIDENT PENCE

> I'm a Christian, a conservative,
> and a Republican, in that order. [54]
> ~ Mike Pence, GOP Convention speech (July 21, 2016)
> Honesty is the axis on which leadership spins. [55]
> ~ Mike Pence (September 8, 2016)

*V*ICE PRESIDENT MIKE PENCE'S POSITION on political issues is fixed, not floating. His evangelical atlas of the past, present, and future world is well known.

Voters should be able to choose between options that are honest and clear. And Mike Pence is crystal clear. He "gave his life to Christ" in 1978, has been married once (in 1985), and has three children. He is young(ish) and fit: at 5 foot 10 and 159 pounds, Pence rides a bicycle regularly and a horse occasionally. He once said, "I think Ronald Reagan said the outside of a horse is good for the inside of a man, and it's certainly good for me."[56] (Though Reagan may have said it too, it was actually a Winston Churchill quote.)

His political viewpoint may be different from yours, but it is internally consistent: He is against

LGBT rights, abortion, needle exchanges, birthright citizenship, and excess government spending. He does not support reducing greenhouse gas emissions from power plants, and he says global warming is a myth. He has said he is for conservatism with a small "c" – limited government, legal gun ownership, conversion therapy to "heal" gay people, and defunding Planned Parenthood.

Mike Pence is a refreshing change from shape-shifting "Biff" Trump, who has reversed himself and his policies countless times over the years and is a lover of tautology. Just as "Biff" abandons people he no longer cares for, he'll often abandon a half-finished sentence in favor of a new and better one, orphaning poor verbs or objects – or even sense.

On election day, it is important that citizens fully and factually understand the candidates and the policies they are voting for. This would be straightforward with Mike Pence, who is honest and upfront about his unwavering beliefs. He must surely think that "Biff's" mastery of "pitchcraft" is more akin to witchcraft than to politics – and Pence would not engage in either practice.

Vice President Mike Pence is consistent and emotionally stable, not prone to cauterization or comedy. The lofty language that other presidents use to inspire may not come naturally to him, but neither would he encourage his followers to throw tomatoes from the cheap seats or practice "terrorism by tweet" as "Biff" Trump does.

Residents of Small Town USA: Mike Pence is your guy. Born and raised in Indiana, Pence truly understands red America, whereas "Biff" lived in the blue state of New York his entire life (part-time in purple Florida). Mike's a nice Hoosier, "Biff" is a bluff bruiser.

Residents of blue cities and blue states: You disagree with a lot of what Mike Pence believes, but clear choices are better than muddled chaos. You will have the opportunity to campaign against Pence's policies with clear arguments and facts without tweetstorms.

We need to have, hold, and fight for a clear, cleansing election to purge the poison of the past and return to the hard work of government by democracy.

When I look back at 2016, in my heart of hearts I wish that Mike Pence or Ted Cruz or John Kasich had run against Bernie Sanders. Because then we could have spent six months arguing and debating the details of health care and social policy instead of being dragged through the mud of email servers, marital infidelities, and bullying.

Bernie would have pitched universal health care, and Ted would have fought to repeal the Affordable Care Act; Bernie would have promised to break up "too big to fail" banks, and Jeb Bush would have campaigned on banks' behalf to remove consumer protections; Bernie would have increased income tax rates, and John Kasich would have tried to cut them.

And of course, the Russians, with their hatred of Clinton and their penchant for Trump, wouldn't have been involved because any of these candidates would have recognized the threat and fought to contain it. We wouldn't have experienced the conflict of a president who appeases Russia despite the cold shoulder of his own party. Republicans and Democrats could have united against a common enemy. Instead, "Biff" identified the *Democratic Party* as the enemy, a strategy that has pitted neighbor against neighbor across their garden fences. As a result, the campaigns served no one while distracting everyone from the serious issues at stake. We wanted an election. Instead we got a circus.

I'm not telling you to vote for Pence. I'm just saying that the next time around, we ought to recognize that the Democratic and Republican parties are not *de facto* enemies. They must vigorously debate the issues that face the nation and put their policies before the electorate. Then, when the counting is over, the winning party forms a government which, because of our system of checks and balances, is held to task by the losing party. That is the way the American democracy works. Instead we have a president who nurtures division, who scolds, bullies, and belittles opponents, and who behaves like a dictator, seemingly unaware that he has lived his whole life in a democracy.

For some contrarian reason, "Biff" stretches his arm around Putin's shoulder when neither his party nor the Democrats nor the American people want that. You can be sure that Mike Pence would not embrace Putin. Neither would Mike Pence insult his opponents; he is not a bully. Mike Pence has released all of his tax returns from the past ten years – there are no secrets lurking in the footnotes or the fine print.. We know who this man is, what he supports, and what he opposes. He is who he seems to be.

Pence stands in the wings ready for the American people or Congress to wake up and give "Biff" his marching orders. He waits loyally and patiently, biding his time and biting his lip. As he once whispered to his friend Jeff Flake, "Just because I'm a-clappin' for it, doesn't mean I'm a-votin' for it."[57]

GUIDE *TO THE* MOVIES

References and timecodes mentioned in the book

Back to the Future Part I

00:06:08
(1985)
Hill Valley, the setting of all three BTTF movies. Here, outside city limits, we see the suburban sprawl typical of the 1980s, with many fast food and retail franchises.

00:06:27
(1985)
Downtown Hill Valley: run-down, dirty, many asphalt parking lots, but few pedestrians.

00:07:15
(1985)
Principal Strickland's first appearance.

00:09:05
(1985)
Downtown Hill Valley: businesses include Cupid's Adult Books, a bail bondsman's office; some storefronts are boarded up or going out of business or have already relocated to Twin Pines Mall.

00:11:57
(1985)
Lyon Estates: the subdivision where the McFly family lives. Shabby, with some litter and graffiti.

00:12:28
(1985)
Biff Tannen's first appearance. He's a mid-level manager in this timeline and is at the McFly home berating and blaming Marty's father George and offloading his work on him. Biff helps himself to George's candy dish and his beer.

00:35:23
(1955)
Lyon Estates: In 1955, developers have just broken ground on the subdivision where the McFly family will later live. A road sign notes that it's two miles from Hill Valley.

00:11:30
(1955)
Hill Valley downtown, circa 1955. A bustling town center with clean streets, a full-service gas station, a malt shop, and many pedestrians.

00:36:50
(1955)
Hill Valley's welcome sign, with logos of numerous local service organizations.

00:37:21
(1955)
Hill Valley: Marty says of the 1955 town, "It's got to be a dream."

00:38:52
(1955)
Biff makes his first appearance as a young man in 1955. His goons are with him. He berates George, offloads his homework on him, then smacks him.

01:00:21
(1955)
Biff harasses Lorraine in the school cafeteria.

01:01:10
(1955)
Biff: "Make like a tree and get out of here."

01:20:24
(1955)
Biff assaults Lorraine in the car in the parking lot during the school dance.

01:23:00
(1955)
Biff shoves Lorraine to the ground and laughs; George delivers a knock-out punch.

01:42:39
(1985)
When Marty returns to 1985, Biff isn't the mid-level manager that he was at the beginning of the movie. He's now merely a lowly auto detailer and he is busily waxing George McFly's car in the driveway.

Back to the Future Part II

00:40:05
(1985A)
"Hell" Valley: the Lyon Estates entry gates have changed and now display "Proud Member of BiffCo Family" along the bottom. BiffCo "For Sale" signs are posted at many houses.

00:41:32
(1985A)
"Hell" Valley: Crashed, burning cars are in the street, including an abandoned police cruiser. Sounds of screaming and gunfire are heard and chalk outlines of bodies are visible.

00:42:05
(1985A)
"Hell" Valley: Mr. Strickland, armed with a shotgun, confronts Marty outside his home. We learn the school burned down six years ago. A gang drives by and fires automatic weapons.

00:43:36
(1985A)
Hill Valley's welcome sign reads "Hell" Valley.

00:43:40
(1985A)
"Hell" Valley's downtown is filled with sex shops and a biker gang.

00:43:50
(1985A)
"Hell" Valley: Exterior of Biff Tannen's Pleasure Paradise, with his face and name on front. It's surrounded by chaos, pollution, and an armored tank.

00:44:43
(1985A)
The Biff Tannen Museum: learn how Biff became one of the richest and most powerful men in America.

00:45:43
(1985A)
Biff: "I just want to say one thing: "God bless America."

00:45:53
(1985A)
Biff and Lorraine's wedding day: "Third time's a charm."

00:46:51
(1985A)
Lorraine's first appearance in alternate reality.

00:47:20
(1985A)
Biff's first appearance as the rich and powerful casino owner.

00:47:29
(1985A)
Lorraine: dressed like a pageant queen, but drinking and quite obviously unhappy.

00:48:05
(1985A)
Biff throws Lorraine to the floor.

00:48:18
(1985A)
Biff punches Marty.

00:48:28
(1985A)
Lorraine says she's leaving Biff; he threatens to cut off and jail her children.

00:48:43
(1985A)
Lorraine at the top of the penthouse stairs.

00:55:42
(1985A)
Biff in the penthouse hot tub with two much younger beauties but not his wife, Lorraine.

00:56:28
(1985A)
Gray's Sports Almanac confrontation between Marty and Biff.

00:56:42
(1985A)
Biff's office in the penthouse.

00:58:45
(1985A)
Biff stands in front of his portrait, looking very Trump-like.

01:00:31
(1985A)
Biff: "Kid, I own the police."

01:02:03
(1955)
Hill Valley: A Lyon Estates billboard advertises the groundbreaking of the suburban development.

01:04:43
(1955)
Biff takes a ball from little kids, taunts them, then tosses the ball onto a roof.

01:05:22
(1955)
Biff argues with a mechanic about the auto repair bill.

01:06:11
(1955)
Hill Valley's downtown is friendly and clean; small businesses line the street.

01:06:12
(1955)
Biff runs up behind Lorraine and lifts her skirt, saying "I think you'd look better wearing nothing at all."

01:06:48
(1955)
Biff: "That's about as funny as a screen door on a battleship."

01:07:00
(1955)
Biff angrily grabs Lorraine by the shoulders and shakes her,
then chases her, insisting that she be his girl.

01:08:25
(1955)
Gray's Sports Almanac: Old Biff (from 2015) delivers the
almanac to his younger self in 1955.

01:08:50
(1955)
Biff: "Now why don't you make like a tree and get outta
here."

01:33:05
(1955)
Gray's Sports Almanac: Marty retrieves the almanac from Biff.

01:36:18
(1955)
Gray's Sports Almanac: As Marty burns the almanac, the
future is set back onto its rightful course. A matchbook
reading "Biff's Pleasure Paradise" changes to "Auto Detailing"
and newspaper headlines return to normal.

Back to the Future Part III

0:14:55
(1885)
Mad Dog Tannen shot a newspaper editor after he'd printed
an unfavorable story about Tannen in 1884.

00:55:16
(1885)
Marshal Strickland's first appearance.

00:55:25
(1885)
Marshal Strickland to Tannen: "Just like you, Tannen, I take every advantage I can get."

00:59:27
(1885)
Mad Dog Tannen: "What's wrong, dude, you yellow?"

01:01:05
(1885)
Tannen: "I'll hunt you and shoot you down like a duck."

01:21:50
(1885)
Mad Dog Tannen doesn't know the word "forfeit" and needs help counting to 10.

SEE FOR YOURSELF

They even look like each other!

Both have orange skin.
Both have golden hair.
Both have bad comb-overs.
Both say they are 6'3" tall.
Both are physically large.
Both are ill-mannered.
Both are egotistical, power-hungry, selfish.
Both are bullies.
Both are womanizers often seen with scantily-clad women.
Both are sexists who disrespect, control, and abuse women.
Both respect no one but themselves.
Both are wealthy and love money.
Both live in tacky-opulent palaces.
Both prefer oversized, gilded furnishings that display wealth.
Both blame others.
Both are loud, blustery, and boastful.
Both lack intelligence.
Neither values reading, is seen with or talks about books.
Both watch a lot of TV.
Both are name-callers and love insults like "loser."
Neither is unafraid of using physical violence.
Both threaten the media.
Both make fun of the weak and vulnerable.
Both mangle words and sayings.
Both take credit for work that isn't theirs.
Each is married to wife #3.
Both own towering casino(s).
Both have wives who are quasi-prisoners.
Both use hyperbole to describe themselves
    (or it's used to describe them).
Both are among the "richest and most
    powerful men in America."
Both have top-floor penthouses in their casinos.

Both name their companies after themselves.
Both plaster that name on everything.
Both are willing to damage the environment for profit.
Both are conmen who profit at others' expense.
Both lobby for policies that benefit themselves.
Both got a "helpful" financial start.
Both ruin cities with their casinos.
Both are called "America's Greatest Living Folk Hero"
Both let henchmen do their dirty work. Biff has his gang;
    Trump's goons rough up protesters and remove
    disobedient participants.
Each commissioned a massive portrait and
    then posed in front of it.
In the BTTF movies and in real life,
    Russia makes the headlines.

They even sound like each other!

Biff: Hello? Anybody home? Think, McFly, think!

Trump: How stupid are the people of Iowa?

Biff: I wanna know who's gonna pay for THIS!

Trump: Who is going to pay for the wall?

Biff: That'll teach him.

Trump: Shoot the bastard (teach them a lesson)!

Biff: How would you like to be rich? I said sure.

Trump: I'm very rich

Biff: Your old man is still a loser. Loser with a capital L!

Trump: Loser!

Biff: Idiot

Trump: Idiot named Glenn Beck, this idiot Woodward

Mad Dog: One day you're going to get a bullet in your back

Trump: I know all about knives and belt buckles

Biff : Hey McFly, your shoe's untied [slaps him]

Trump: He's not a war hero

Biff: I'm gonna take it outta your ass... Hold him, guys.

Trump: I would bomb the shit out of them.

Biff: Irish bug!

Trump: Bad hombres

Biff: Make like a tree and get outta here

Trump: I have words, the best words!

Biff sidekick : Let's lock him in that trunk!

Trump sidekick: Manigault-Newman ... repeatedly mentioned how she was "locked" into the conference room. She accused General Kelly of "false imprisonment."

Mad Dog: you gutless yellow pie-slinger

Trump: Pocahontas bombed last night!

Biff: Kid, I own the police.

Trump sidekick: The president's power will not be questioned.

Trump: I have absolute right to do what I want to do with the Justice Department.

Biff: I just want to say one thing: God bless America!

Trump: God bless America!

Additional Reading

I Imagine. (2015, November 11). Back to the Future - Donald Trump. Retrieved from youtube.com/watch?v=bOrhnWgOFGg&app=desktop

S. (2017, October 21). A Chronological History of the Hill Valley Telegraph - Part I. Retrieved from newspapersinfiction.wordpress.com/2015/04/03/a-chronological-history-of-the-hill-valley-telegraph-part-i/

Abadi, M. (2017, November 30). Trump has used some bizarre words and phrases that left people scratching their heads - here are 8 of the worst. Retrieved from businessinsider.com/trump-made-up-words-confusing-phrases-2017-11#bad-hombres-8

Abdul-Jabbar, K. (2016, February 01). Dear Trump supporters: Hear me out before you vote. Yours, Kareem Abdul-Jabbar. Retrieved from washingtonpost.com/posteverything/wp/2016/02/01/dear-trump-supporters-hear-me-out-before-you-vote-yours-kareem-abdul-jabbar/

Ahmed, T. (2017, September 20). Renowned primatologist Jane Goodall thinks Trump is like an aggressive chimp. Retrieved from newsweek.com/donald-trump-aggressive-chimp-and-may-not-last-long-668128

Avery, B. (2018, April 6). The Nostalgia Trap: The memory lane politics of Steven ... Retrieved from vanyaland.com/2018/04/06/the-nostalgia-trap-the-memory-lane-politics-of-steven-spielberg/

Back to the Future trilogy. (n.d.). Retrieved September 21, 2018, from backtothefuture.wikia.com/wiki/Back_to_the_Future_trilogy

Barrón-López, L., & Delaney, A. (2015, July 20). Donald Trump Is Biff Tannen From 'Back To The Future'. Retrieved from huffingtonpost.com/entry/donald-trump-is-biff-tannen_us_55a94b67e4b065dfe89e414c

Benen, S. (2018, August 14). What Trump's McCain snub tells us about his character. Retrieved from msnbc.com/rachel-maddow-show/what-trumps-mccain-snub-tells-us-about-his-character?cid=sm_fb_maddow

Berkowitz, J. (2017, January 13). This Newly Surfaced 1950s TV Show Eerily Predicted Trump, and So Did These 5 Others. Retrieved from fastcompany.com/3067216/newly-surfaced-1950s-tv-show-eerily-predicted-trump-and-so-did-these-5-others

Bloomberg News. (2018, April 16). Industry has reservations about Trump hotels. Retrieved from finance-commerce.com/2018/04/industry-has-reservations-about-trump-hotels/

Bornstein Letters of Health for Trump. (2017, February 02). Retrieved from nytimes.com/interactive/2017/02/01/us/politics/document-Bornstein-Letter-of-Health-for-Trump.html

Brayson, J. (2016, November 9). The Worst of 'Back to the Future 2' Is Now Reality. Retrieved from bustle.com/articles/194394-how-back-to-the-future-2s-alternate-timeline-basically-predicted-donald-trump

Bttfcom. (2010, November 13). Complete 'Biff Tannen Museum' video monitor footage revealed - a BacktotheFuture.com exclusive. Retrieved from youtube.com/watch?v=lhjANIyY0Sw&feature=youtu.be

Burleigh, N. (2018, March 23). How Donald Trump Rules America's Garden of Dicks and Sparked the #MeToo Movement. Retrieved from newsweek.com/2017/11/17/me-

too-donald-trump-harvey-weinstein-powerful-predators-
facing-accusers-704658.html

Campbell, W. W., & U.S. Army. (2016, February 03). History
shows businessmen make bad presidents. Retrieved from
thehill.com/blogs/congress-blog/presidential-
campaign/262749-history-shows-businessmen-make-bad-
presidents

Cdisalv. (2015, July 25). Donald Trump 2016! Retrieved from
youtube.com/watch?v=cKgQdffJmbc

Chait, J. (2018, August 30). Coastal Snob Trump Mocks
Sessions' Alabama Accent, Degree. Retrieved from
nymag.com/daily/intelligencer/2018/08/coastal-snob-trump-
mocks-sessions-alabama-accent-degree.html

Charney, N. (2017, May 08). The art of the art of Trump: A
critical reading of "The Visionary," that painting of him at
Mar-a-Lago. Retrieved from salon.com/2017/05/07/the-art-of-
the-art-of-trump-a-critical-reading-of-the-visionary-that-
painting-of-him-at-mar-a-lago/

ChrisvanvlietDOTtv. (2016, November 22). 'Back to the Future
2' director predicted Donald Trump as president in 1989.
Retrieved from youtube.com/watch?v=CPfxbQZvv7Q

Cohen, E. A. (2018, September 04). How This Will End.
Retrieved from theatlantic.com/ideas/archive/2018/08/the-
end-of-trumps-reign/568480/

DeadHead Animation. (2015, August 11). Was Donald Trump
in Back to the Future? Retrieved from
youtube.com/watch?v=YNvR5HwsBEc

Deprez, E. E., Green, J., Niquette, M., & Young, E. (2017,
May 17). How Trump's Rust Belt Voters Have Changed Since
the Election. Retrieved from bloomberg.com/features/2017-
trump-heartland-sentiment/

Dodds, L. (2015, October 21). Who was John Titor, the 'time traveller' who came from 2036 to warn us of a nuclear war? Retrieved from telegraph.co.uk/news/science/11945420/Who-was-John-Titor-the-time-traveller-who-came-from-2036-to-warn-us-of-a-nuclear-war.html

Donnelly, M. (2018, June 30). Tim Robbins Says America's Living a Bad Version of 'Back to the Future' – and Trump is Biff. Retrieved from sfgate.com/entertainment/the-wrap/article/Tim-Robbins-Says-America-s-Living-a-Bad-Version-13038823.php

Editorial. (2015, December 30). Biff strikes back: Trump sees the enemy, and it is us | New Hampshire. Retrieved from newhampshire.com/Biff-strikes-back-Trump-sees-the-enemy-and-it-is-us

Feldman, J. (2015, September 3). Trump Tower Guard Allegedly Hits Protester in Heated Scuffle - Mediaite. Retrieved from mediaite.com/online/trump-tower-security-guard-punches-protester-in-the-face/

Five Dollar Feminist. (2017, December 29). Come and Get Your Donald Trump Word Salad with Dementia Dressing! Retrieved from wonkette.com/come-and-get-your-donald-trump-word-salad-with-dementia-dressing

Freeman, H. (2016, November 21). Christopher Lloyd: Donald Trump's a beast. He needs to be put in a cage. Retrieved from theguardian.com/film/2016/nov/21/christopher-lloyd-donald-trumps-a-beast-he-needs-to-be-put-in-a-cage

French, D. (2016, March 15). Donald Trump Is No King David: It's Time for Christians to Take a Stand. Retrieved from nationalreview.com/2016/03/donald-trump-christian-supporters-its-time-take-stand-against-trump/

Friedersdorf, C. (2016, September 26). Donald Trump Is Senselessly Cruel. Retrieved from theatlantic.com/politics/archive/2016/09/donald-trumps-cruel-streak/501554/

Futurepedia. Retrieved from backtothefuture.wikia.com/wiki/Main_Page

Grdodd12. (2015, August 19). TRUMP / TANNEN 2016 | (Back to the future spoof). Retrieved from youtube.com/watch?v=useBId2qYXM

Haberman, M. (2015, December 28). Donald Trump Calls Newspaper Publisher a 'Lowlife' and Assails Chris Christie. Retrieved from nytimes.com/politics/first-draft/2015/12/28/donald-trump-calls-newspaper-publisher-a-lowlife-and-assails-chris-christie/

Hains, T. (2016, May 3). Ted Cruz Compares Donald Trump to Villain from Back to the Future. Retrieved from realclearpolitics.com/video/2016/05/03/ted_cruz_compares_d onald_trump_to_villain_from_back_to_the_future.html

Handy, B. (2016, November 01). An Illustrated History of Donald Trump's Hair. Warning! Don't Read Before Lunch! Retrieved from vanityfair.com/news/photos/2015/09/an-illustrated-history-of-donald-trumps-hair

Hannon, E. (2018, August 30). In the Trumpiest of Trump Moves, Trump Reportedly Asked Disgraced Spousal Abuser Rob Porter to Become White House Counsel Last Year. Retrieved from slate.com/news-and-politics/2018/08/trump-reportedly-asked-disgraced-spousal-abuser-rob-porter-to-become-white-house-counsel-last-year.html

Healy, P., & Haberman, M. (2015, December 05). 95,000 Words, Many of Them Ominous, from Donald Trump's Tongue. Retrieved from nytimes.com/2015/12/06/us/politics/95000-words-many-of-them-ominous-from-donald-trumps-tongue.html

Heanue, S. (2017, March 17). What influences Trump's gaudy taste? Look to King Louis XIV. Retrieved from abc.net.au/news/2017-03-17/donald-trump-decor-is-inspired-by-french-king-louis-xiv/8364220

Hines, A. (2018, September 18). Donald Trump's chaotic use of metaphor is a crucial part of his appeal. Retrieved from theconversation.com/donald-trumps-chaotic-use-of-metaphor-is-a-crucial-part-of-his-appeal-61383

Hitchcock, M. (2015, October 26). 'Back to the Future' A Fantasy That Addresses Real-Life ... Retrieved from goodmenproject.com/arts/back-to-the-future-a-fantasy-that-addresses-real-life-issues-of-bullying-masculinity-and-sexual-assault-knts/

Hutchisson, S. K. (2016, August 9). The Similarities Between Biff Tannen and Donald Trump. Retrieved from theodysseyonline.com/the-similarities-between-biff-tannen-and-donald-trump

Newkirk II, V. R. (2018, August 17). Trump Can't Even Honor Aretha Franklin Properly. Retrieved from theatlantic.com/politics/archive/2018/08/aretha-franklin-trump/567760/

IOTrendz. (2015, October 24). Back to the Future Writer Says Biff Was Based On Donald Trump. Retrieved from youtube.com/watch?v=EUHRf-cqfSU

Jamesmontalbano. (2015, June 26). Trump to The Future. Retrieved from youtube.com/watch?v=B_iL8TtPOt0

Johnson, D. K. (2018, May 26). How Trump Is Improving (and Ruining) Science Fiction. Retrieved from psychologytoday.com/us/blog/plato-pop/201805/how-trump-is-improving-and-ruining-science-fiction

Johnston, C. (2016, April 20). Proof We're Living in the Back to the Future Universe. Retrieved from cracked.com/video_19964_why-donald-trump-new-bad-guy-from-back-to-future.html

Joyner, A. (2018, September 19). What Would a Mike Pence Presidency Look Like? Retrieved from newsweek.com/president-mike-pence-heres-what-his-administration-would-look-1125735

Keneally, M. (2018, February 22). List of Trump's accusers and their allegations of sexual misconduct. Retrieved from abcnews.go.com/Politics/list-trumps-accusers-allegations-sexual-misconduct/story?id=51956410

Koffler, J. (2015, August 07). Donald Trump: 16 Successful and Unsuccessful Business Ventures. Retrieved from time.com/3988970/donald-trump-business/

Kruse, M. (2015, August 14). The 199 Most Donald Trump Things Donald Trump Has Ever Said. Retrieved from politico.com/magazine/story/2015/08/the-absolute-trumpest-121328

Kurtzman, D. (2018, August 2). Stupid Donald Trump Quotes. Retrieved from thoughtco.com/donald-trump-quotes-2733859

Kyff, R. (2017, February 21). Word Watch: Trump the Master of Metaphors. Retrieved from courant.com/features/hc-president-trumps-metaphors-20170225-story.html

Lakoff, G. (2016, August 19). Understanding Trump. Retrieved from georgelakoff.com/2016/07/23/understanding-trump-2/

Lanzendorfer, J. (2016, November 18). How Reality TV Made Donald Trump President. Retrieved from vice.com/en_us/article/avak5a/how-reality-tv-made-donald-trump-president

Levitz, E., & Walsh, J. D. (2018, January 08). Trump's Greatest Worst Hits of 2017. Retrieved from nymag.com/daily/intelligencer/2018/01/donald-trump-greatest-worst-hits-of-2017.html

Lozada, C. (2015, August 05). Donald Trump on women, sex, marriage and feminism. Retrieved from washingtonpost.com/news/book-party/wp/2015/08/05/donald-trump-on-women-sex-marriage-and-feminism/?utm_term=.f907c6bc19ee

Madrick, J. (2016, August 10). Donald Trump Spreads Economic Fairy Dust. Retrieved from thenation.com/article/donald-trump-spreads-economic-fairy-dust/

Major, R. (n.d.). America Worships the Sham-Messiah. Retrieved September 21, 2018, from versopolis.com/column/357/america-worships-the-sham-messiah

Martinez, A. (2017, March 29). Who Said It: Donald Trump or Biff Tannen? Retrieved from playbuzz.com/alejandram13/who-said-it-donald-trump-of-biff-tannen

Mascaro, L. (2016, September 12). 'Believe me': People say Trump's language is affecting political discourse 'bigly'. Retrieved from .latimes.com/politics/la-na-pol-trump-language-20160912-snap-story.html

Mathis-Lilley, B. (2016, April 25). A Continually Growing List of Violent Incidents at Trump Events. Retrieved from slate.com/blogs/the_slatest/2016/03/02/a_list_of_violent_inci dents_at_donald_trump_rallies_and_events.html

Matthews, D. (2017, January 19). Trump's books reveal there is so much more beneath the insults he hurls. Retrieved from vox.com/a/donald-trump-books

McCormick, J. C. (2018, April 06). Cinema's Ultimate Jerks #12: Biff Tannen (Back to the Future). Retrieved from goombastomp.com/cuj-biff/

McKay, D. (2017, August 8). The president behind the wheel of the DeLorean | Overland ... Retrieved from overland.org.au/2017/08/the-president-behind-the-wheel-of-the-delorean/

Mcwhorter, J. (2018, February 06). What Trump's Speech Says About His Mental Fitness. Retrieved from nytimes.com/interactive/2018/02/06/opinion/trump-speech-mental-capacity.html

Megan Hitchcock. (2016, June 12). Retrieved from thelegalgeeks.com/2015/10/26/a-lesson-in-anti-bullying-demonstrated-by-our-favorite-bully-biff-tannen-from-back-to-the-future/

Merelli, A. (2016, October 17). Clinton's new ad uses Biff from "Back to the Future" to remind Americans how to spot a bully. Retrieved from qz.com/811155/donald-trump-back-to-the-future-mean-girls-hillary-clintons-new-ad-features-the-biggest-bullies-in-american-pop-culture/

Mikkelson, D. (2016, August 1). Donald Trump's Bankruptcies. Retrieved from snopes.com/news/2016/08/01/donald-trumps-bankruptcies/

Mudde, C. (2016, December 20). Why nostalgia dominated the politics of 2016. Retrieved from newsweek.com/1950s-1930s-racism-us-europe-nostalgia-cas-mudde-531546

Mullins, P. (2016, December 29). The Triumph of Tackiness: The Materiality of Trump. Retrieved from paulmullins.wordpress.com/2016/11/22/the-triumph-of-tackiness-the-materiality-of-trump/

Murphy-Gill, M. (2017, January 19). The faith of Donald Trump. Retrieved from uscatholic.org/articles/201701/faith-donald-trump-30910

Nussbaum, E. (2018, May 31). The TV That Created Donald Trump. Retrieved from newyorker.com/magazine/2017/07/31/the-tv-that-created-donald-trump

Ordo, M. (2016, November 24). A Trump look-alike in Back to the Future II. Retrieved from sfchronicle.com/entertainment/article/A-Trump-look-alike-in-Back-to-the-Future-II-10634777.php

Parker, R. (2016, July 28). Ted Cruz Warns of "Biff Tannen Presidency" if Donald Trump Is Elected. Retrieved from hollywoodreporter.com/news/ted-cruz-likens-a-trump-890311

Peyser, E. (2018, August 17). Of Course Donald Trump Hates Dogs. Retrieved from vice.com/en_us/article/7xqqb4/of-course-donald-trump-hates-dogs-vgtrn?utm_source=dmfb

Pieper, C., & Henderson, M. (2016, November 06). 10 reasons you can't be a Christian and vote for Donald Trump. dallasnews.com/opinion/commentary/2016/02/29/pieper-and-henderson-10-reasons-you-cant-be-a-christian-and-vote-for-donald-trump

Plante, C. (2015, July 27). The Back to the Future Donald Trump mash-up is too real and too terrifying. Retrieved from theverge.com/2015/7/27/9047761/back-to-the-future-donald-trump-video

Politico Magazine. (2016, November 05). The 155 Craziest Things Trump Said This Election. Retrieved from politico.com/magazine/story/2016/11/the-155-craziest-things-trump-said-this-cycle-214420

Quealy, K. (2016, December 06). How to Know What Donald Trump Really Cares About: Look at What He's Insulting. nytimes.com/interactive/2016/12/06/upshot/how-to-know-what-donald-trump-really-cares-about-look-at-who-hes-insulting.html

Roberts, R. (2016, April 28). I sat next to Donald Trump at the infamous 2011 White House correspondents' dinner. Retrieved from washingtonpost.com/lifestyle/style/i-sat-next-to-donald-trump-at-the-infamous-2011-white-house-correspondents-dinner/2016/04/27/5cf46b74-0bea-11e6-8ab8-9ad050f76d7d_story.html

Rose, S. (2016, February 14). From Back to the Future's Biff to Donald Trump: How pop culture can make a president. Retrieved from theguardian.com/film/2016/feb/14/pop-culture-make-us-president-donald-trump-biff-back-to-the-future

Shafer, J. (2018, July 16). Some Dare Call It Treason. Retrieved from politico.com/magazine/story/2018/07/16/some-dare-call-it-treason-219014

Shiny. (2016, November 07). An Open Letter to Donald J. Trump, Evil Time Traveler. Retrieved from medium.com/@mr_shiny/an-open-letter-to-donald-j-trump-evil-time-traveler-e712d36687da

M. L. (2015, September 3). Should Trump Have Indexed? Retrieved from bloomberg.com/view/articles/2015-09-03/should-donald-trump-have-indexed-

Silverman, G. (2017, April 13). How the Bible Belt lost God and found Trump. Retrieved from ft.com/content/b41d0ee6-1e96-11e7-b7d3-163f5a7f229c

Smith, E. B. (2016, August 02). Proof Warren Buffett is right about Donald Trump being a lousy investor. Retrieved from marketwatch.com/story/buffett-puts-money-on-monkey-to-outperform-trump-as-an-investor-2016-08-02

Smokler, K. (2015, July 02). I went "Back to the Future" but nothing was there: How I lost Hill Valley and where I found it. Retrieved from salon.com/2015/07/02/i_went_back_to_the_future_but_nothing_was_there_how_i_lost_hill_valley_and_where_i_found_it/

Stalter, K. (2016, September 01). Would Donald Trump Be Better Off Investing In Stocks? Retrieved from forbes.com/sites/katestalter/2016/09/01/would-donald-trump-be-better-off-investing-in-stocks/#2f58d7bc437b

Stuart, T. (2018, June 25). 'Back to the Future' Writer: Biff Is Donald Trump. Retrieved from rollingstone.com/politics/politics-news/back-to-the-future-writer-biff-is-donald-trump-190408/

Taibbi, M. (2018, June 25). The Madness of Donald Trump. Retrieved from rollingstone.com/politics/politics-features/the-madness-of-donald-trump-197853/

Thomas, R. E. (2018, March 26). Trump and Biden Challenged Each Other to Fisticuffs. Retrieved from elle.com/culture/career-politics/a19562181/trump-and-biden-fight/

Thornton, P. (2015, October 21). What 'Back to the Future' didn't predict: Neighborhoods off-limits to the middle class. Retrieved from latimes.com/opinion/livable-city/la-ol-back-to-the-future-south-pasadena-20151021-story.html

Tully, S., & Parloff, R. (2016, April 21). Business the Trump Way. Retrieved from fortune.com/donald-trump-businessman/

Tuttle, I. (2016, February 19). The Litigious - and Bullying - Mr. Trump. Retrieved from nationalreview.com/2016/02/donald-trump-tim-obrien-courtroom-story/

Wagner, J. (2016, October 17). New Clinton ad places Trump in tradition of big-screen bullies like Biff from 'Back to the Future'. Retrieved from washingtonpost.com/news/post-politics/wp/2016/10/17/new-clinton-ad-places-trump-in-tradition-of-big-screen-bullies-like-biff-from-back-to-the-future/

Waldman, P. (2016, December 13). Donald Trump, the all-knowing know-nothing. Retrieved from theweek.com/articles/666931/donald-trump-allknowing-knownothing

Walker, B. (2018, February 14). Time Travelin' Trump – Benjamen Walker – Medium. Retrieved from medium.com/@benjamenwalker/time-travelin-trump-d891ba95ddcb

Walker, J. (2016, March 14). The Trump Administration Is a Sinkhole of Sleaze. Retrieved from reason.com/archives/2018/08/09/the-trump-administration-is-a-sinkhole-o

Weinberg, M. (2018, February 27). What I Learned Watching 'Back to the Future' With Ronald Reagan. Retrieved from politico.com/magazine/story/2018/02/27/ronald-reagan-press-aide-movie-nights-with-reagan-217095

Wilhelm, H. (2015, October 23). The Biff Tannen presidency. chicagotribune.com/news/opinion/commentary/ct-joe-biden-donald-trump-hillary-clinton-perspec-1023-jm-20151023-story.html

Zaru, D. (2017, August 17). Paper: Trump is Biff from 'Back to the Future'. cnn.com/2015/12/28/politics/donald-trump-biff-back-to-the-future/

Zuckerman, P. (2016, October 12). Trump's Sexism Is Deeply Biblical. Retrieved from psychologytoday.com/us/blog/the-secular-life/201610/trumps-sexism-is-deeply-biblical

It's Morning in America Again: How Reagan set the foundation for Trump. Retrieved from politicsofnostalgia.com/its-morning-in-america-again-how-reagan-set-foundation-for-trump/

WORKS CITED

Additional sources used for this book

@realdonaldtrump. (2018, March 22). Crazy Joe Biden is trying to act like a tough guy. Retrieved from twitter.com/realdonaldtrump/status/976765417908776963

Anonymous. (2018, September 05). I Am Part of the Resistance Inside the Trump Administration. Retrieved from nytimes.com/2018/09/05/opinion/trump-white-house-anonymous-resistance.html

Associated Press. (2017, May 25). Raw: Trump Pushes Past Montenegro PM at NATO. Retrieved from youtube.com/watch?v=Iimj0j4NYME

Back to the Future Part 2 (7/12) Movie CLIP - Biff's World (1989) HD. (2011, June 16). Retrieved from youtube.com/watch?v=S4m848bh1iY

Baynes, C. (2018, June 29). Trump yanked around by Portuguese president during vigorous handshake. Retrieved from independent.co.uk/news/world/americas/trump-handshake-portugal-president-rebelo-de-sousa-white-house-a8422741.html

Bixby, S. (2016, March 04). Trump: 'I could have told Mitt Romney to drop to his knees' – as it happened. Retrieved from theguardian.com/us-news/live/2016/mar/03/campaign-updates-us-presidential-election-2016-gop-debate-romney-trump-clinton

Brayson, J. (2018, April 25). The Worst of 'Back to the Future 2' Is Now Reality. Retrieved from bustle.com/articles/194394-how-back-to-the-future-2s-alternate-timeline-basically-predicted-donald-trump

Carter, G. (1984, May 01). The Secret to Donald Trump's Success. Retrieved from gq.com/story/donald-trump-gq-profile-graydon-carter

Collins, B. (2015, October 21). 'Back to the Future' Writer: Biff Tannen Is Based on Donald Trump. Retrieved from thedailybeast.com/back-to-the-future-writer-biff-tannen-is-based-on-donald-trump

Complete 'Biff Tannen Museum' video monitor footage revealed - a BacktotheFuture.com exclusive. (2010, November 13). Retrieved from youtube.com/watch?v=lhjANIyY0Sw&feature=youtu.be

Crouch, I. (2018, January 18). The Rise of the Anti-Trump "Girthers". Retrieved from newyorker.com/culture/rabbit-holes/the-rise-of-the-anti-trump-girthers

Diamond, J. (2016, January 24). Donald Trump could 'shoot somebody and not lose voters' - CNNPolitics. Retrieved from cnn.com/2016/01/23/politics/donald-trump-shoot-somebody-support/

Factbase. (2018, August 13). Transcript - Remarks: Donald Trump Delivers a Speech at a Fundraiser in Utica, NY - August 13, 2018. Retrieved from factba.se/transcript/donald-trump-remarks-fundraiser-utica-ny-august-13-2018

FandangoNOW Extras. (2014, March 11). Back to the Future Part III Deleted Scene - The Tannen Gang Kill Marshall Strickland (1990) Movie HD. Retrieved from youtube.com/watch?v=2RYb7GHWuL4

Folley, A. (2018, June 21). Ian Bremmer: Trump tossed candy to Merkel at G-7, said 'don't say I never give you anything'. Retrieved from thehill.com/blogs/blog-briefing-room/news/393311-ian-bremmer-trump-tossed-candy-to-merkel-during-g-7-said-dont

Fuller, J. (2017, October 07). Trump Is the Star of These Bizarre Victorian Novels. Retrieved from politico.com/magazine/story/2017/10/07/baron-trump-novels-victorian-215689

Gabbatt, A. (2018, January 17). A tall tale? Accuracy of Trump's medical report – and new height – questioned. Retrieved from theguardian.com/us-news/2018/jan/17/a-tall-tale-accuracy-of-trumps-medical-report-and-new-height-questioned

Groden, C. (2015, August 20). Donald Trump Would Be Richer If He'd Have Invested in Index Funds. Retrieved from http://fortune.com/2015/08/20/donald-trump-index-funds/

Grynbaum, M. (2017, February 17). Trump Calls the News Media the 'Enemy of the American People'. Retrieved from nytimes.com/2017/02/17/business/trump-calls-the-news-media-the-enemy-of-the-people.html

Hu, E. (2017, September 22). Kim Jong Un Issues Statement On Trump: 'A Frightened Dog Barks Louder'. Retrieved from npr.org/sections/thetwo-way/2017/09/21/552756716/kim-jong-un-issues-statement-on-trump-a-frightened-dog-barks-louder

Keneally, M. (2018, February 22). List of Trump's accusers and their allegations of sexual misconduct. Retrieved from abcnews.go.com/Politics/list-trumps-accusers-allegations-sexual-misconduct/story?id=51956410

Kolata, G. (2013, October 14). In Struggle With Weight, Taft Used a Modern Diet. Retrieved from nytimes.com/2013/10/15/health/in-struggle-with-weight-william-howard-taft-used-a-modern-diet.html

Kruse, M. (2018, June 01). 'He Pretty Much Gave In to Whatever They Asked For'. Retrieved from politico.com/magazine/story/2018/06/01/donald-trump-deals-negotiation-art-of-deal-218584

Lee, M. (2016, September 26). Fact Check: Has Trump declared bankruptcy four or six times? Retrieved from washingtonpost.com/politics/2016/live-updates/general-election/real-time-fact-checking-and-analysis-of-the-first-presidential-debate/fact-check-has-trump-declared-bankruptcy-four-or-six-times

Leinberger, C., & Leinberger, L. (2014, February 28). The Top 12 Movies About Urbanism. Retrieved from nextcity.org/daily/entry/the-top-12-movies-about-urbanism

Lewandowski Defends Trump: 'He's the Greatest Deal-Maker Our Country's Ever Seen'. (2017, April 22). Retrieved from insider.foxnews.com/2017/04/22/corey-lewandowski-president-trump-accomplishments-first-100-days

Mandell, A. (2015, October 21). Believe it: 'Back to the Future' predicted Trump's run. Retrieved from amp.usatoday.com/amp/74359844

Maza, C. (2018, June 20). Donald Trump threw Starbursts at Angela Merkel, saying "Don't say I never give you anything." Retrieved from newsweek.com/donald-trump-threw-starburst-candies-angela-merkel-dont-say-i-never-give-you-987178

McAdams, J. (2018, August 24). Trump's Hair Stylist Granted Immunity – Jay McAdams – Medium. Retrieved from medium.com/@jaymcadams/trumps-hair-stylist-granted-immunity-8af00dd7cf36

Murphy, Bernice. (2010). "You Space Bastard! You Killed my Pines!" Back to the Future, Nostalgia and the Suburban Dream. 49-62.

SAD! Donald 'Biff' Trump Is President

Pool Report - The Guardian. (2016, October 10). Trump 'prowls' behind Clinton during presidential debate – video. Retrieved from theguardian.com/us-news/video/2016/oct/10/donald-trump-behind-hillary-clinton-debate-video

Reilly, S. (2018, April 25). USA TODAY exclusive: Hundreds allege Donald Trump doesn't pay his bills. Retrieved from usatoday.com/story/news/politics/elections/2016/06/09/donald-trump-unpaid-bills-republican-president-laswuits/85297274/

Republican Debate: Read the Transcript of the Primetime Debate. (2015, August 07). time.com/3988276/republican-debate-primetime-transcript-full-text/

Riotta, C. (2017, July 31). Did an author from the 1800s predict the Trumps, Russia and America's downfall? Retrieved from newsweek.com/donald-trump-predicted-ingersoll-lockwood-adventures-barron-melania-last-644284

Romo, V. (2018, March 23). Former 'Playboy' Model Spills Details of Alleged Affair: Trump 'Tried to Pay Me.' Retrieved from npr.org/sections/thetwo-way/2018/03/23/596257288/former-playboy-model-spills-alleged-affair-details-trump-tried-to-pay-her

Schulman, K. (2011, May 11). "The President's Speech" at the White House Correspondents' Dinner. Retrieved from obamawhitehouse.archives.gov/blog/2011/05/01/president-s-speech-white-house-correspondents-dinner

Stuart, T. (2018, June 25). 'Back to the Future' Writer: Biff Is Donald Trump. Retrieved from rollingstone.com/politics/politics-news/back-to-the-future-writer-biff-is-donald-trump-190408/

Stuart, T. (2018, June 25). Timeline of Donald Trump's Creepiness rollingstone.com/politics/politics-features/a-timeline-of-donald-trumps-creepiness-while-he-owned-miss-universe-191860/

Trump, D. J. (2005, September 22). Full Transcript of Interview: Donald Trump on The Howard Stern Show. Retrieved from factba.se/search#She will always be cute

Trump, D. J. (2017, December 21). Donald Trump's Taped Comments About Women. nytimes.com/2016/10/08/us/donald-trump-tape-transcript.html

Watson, K. (2018, May 01). Trump dictated glowing bill of health. cbsnews.com/news/harold-bornstein-donald-trump-dictated-2015-letter/

Willis, A. (2016, November 10). Biff from Back to the Future was based on Donald Trump. Retrieved from metro.co.uk/2016/11/10/back-to-the-futures-biff-tannen-was-based-on-donald-trump-6248039/

Wilson, J. (2018, June 14). Doxxing, assault, death threats: The new dangers facing U.S. journalists covering extremism. Retrieved from theguardian.com/world/2018/jun/14/doxxing-assault-death-threats-the-new-dangers-facing-us-journalists-covering-extremism

York, P. (2017, March/April). Donald Trump Has a "Dictator Chic" Design Taste. politico.com/magazine/story/2017/03/trump-style-dictator-autocrats-design-214877

Zimmerman, N. (2016, October 13). Trump told 14-year-old girl he'd be dating her soon. thehill.com/blogs/blog-briefing-room/news/300928-trump-told-14-year-old-girl-hell-be-dating-her-soon

ENDNOTES

[1] Brayson, J. (2018, April 25). How 'Back to the Future 2's Alternate Timeline Basically Predicted Donald Trump. Retrieved from bustle.com/articles/194394-how-back-to-the-future-2s-alternate-timeline-basically-predicted-donald-trump

[2] Stuart, T. (2018, June 25). 'Back to the Future' Writer: Biff Is Donald Trump. Retrieved from rollingstone.com/politics/politics-news/back-to-the-future-writer-biff-is-donald-trump-190408/

[3] Mandell, A. (2015, October 21). Believe it: 'Back to the Future' predicted Trump's run. Retrieved from usatoday.com/amp/74359844

[4] Collins, B. (2015, October 21). 'Back to the Future' Writer: Biff Tannen Is Based on Donald Trump. Retrieved from thedailybeast.com/back-to-the-future-writer-biff-tannen-is-based-on-donald-trump

[5] Carter, G. (1984, May 01). The Secret to Donald Trump's Success. Retrieved from gq.com/story/donald-trump-gq-profile-graydon-carter

[6] Collins, B. 'Back to the Future' Writer: Biff Tannen Is Based on Donald Trump.

[7] McAdams, J. (2018, August 24). Trump's Hair Stylist Granted Immunity – Jay McAdams – Medium. Retrieved from medium.com/@jaymcadams/trumps-hair-stylist-granted-immunity-8af00dd7cf36

[8] Willis, A. (2016, November 10). Biff from Back to the Future was based on Donald Trump. Retrieved from metro.co.uk/2016/11/10/back-to-the-futures-biff-tannen-was-based-on-donald-trump-6248039/

[9] York, P. (2017, March/April). Donald Trump Has a "Dictator Chic" Design Taste. Retrieved from politico.com/magazine/story/2017/03/trump-style-dictator-autocrats-design-214877

[10] Crouch, I. (2018, January 18). The Rise of the Anti-Trump "Girthers". Retrieved from newyorker.com/culture/rabbit-holes/the-rise-of-the-anti-trump-girthers

[11] Watson, K. (2018, May 01). Trump's longtime doctor says Trump dictated glowing bill of health. Retrieved from cbsnews.com/news/harold-bornstein-donald-trump-dictated-2015-letter/

[12] MOVIECLIPS channel (2011, June 16). Back to the Future Part 2 (7/12) Movie CLIP – Biff's World (1989). Retrieved from youtube.com/watch?v=S4m848bh1iY

[13] BacktotheFuture.com (2010, November 13). Complete 'Biff Tannen Museum' video monitor footage revealed. Retrieved from youtube.com/watch?v=IhjANIyY0Sw&feature=youtu.be

[14] Asshole. (n.d.). Retrieved from merriam-webster.com/dictionary/asshole

[15] Reilly, S. (2018, April 25). USA TODAY exclusive: Hundreds allege Donald Trump doesn't pay his bills. USA Today. usatoday.com/story/news/politics/elections/2016/06/09/donald-trump-unpaid-bills-republican-president-laswuits/85297274/

[16] @realdonaldtrump. (2018, March 22). "Crazy Joe Biden is trying to act like a tough guy" Retrieved from twitter.com/realdonaldtrump/status/976765417908776963

[17] Miller, M. E. (2016, February 23). Donald Trump on a protester: 'I'd like to punch him in the face.' Retrieved from washingtonpost.com/news/morning-mix/wp/2016/02/23/donald-trump-on-protester-id-like-to-punch-him-in-the-face

[18] Jhaveri, H. (2016, October 12). Donald Trump mocks the NFL's 'soft' concussion protocol. Retrieved from ftw.usatoday.com/2016/10/donald-trump-mocks-the-nfls-soft-concussion-protocol

[19] Pool Report, The Guardian. (2016, October 10). Trump 'prowls' behind Clinton during presidential debate – video. Retrieved from theguardian.com/us-news/video/2016/oct/10/donald-trump-behind-hillary-clinton-debate-video

[20] Baynes, C. (2018, June 29). Trump yanked around by Portuguese president during vigorous handshake. Retrieved from independent.co.uk/news/world/americas/trump-handshake-portugal-president-rebelo-de-sousa-white-house-a8422741.html

[21] Associated Press. (2017, May 25). Raw: Trump Pushes Past Montenegro Prime Minister at NATO. Retrieved from https://www.youtube.com/watch?v=Iimj0j4NYME

[22] Bixby, S. (2016, March 04). Trump: 'I could have told Mitt Romney to drop to his knees.' Retrieved from theguardian.com/us-news/live/2016/mar/03/campaign-updates-us-presidential-election-2016-gop-debate-romney-trump-clinton

[23] The Daily Beast. (2015, August 07). Watch: Trump Told Female 'Apprentice' to 'Drop to Your Knees'. Retrieved from thedailybeast.com/watch-trump-told-female-apprentice-to-drop-to-your-knees

[24] Colvin, J. (2018, January 07). Trump says he's 'like, really smart,' and 'a very stable genius.' Retrieved from apnews.com/2bb960fda0264c488d454632628cb193

[25] Trump, D. J. (2017, December 21). Transcript: Donald Trump's Taped Comments About Women. Retrieved from nytimes.com/2016/10/08/us/donald-trump-tape-transcript.html

[26] Trump, D. J. (2005, September 22). Full Transcript of Interview: Donald Trump on The Howard Stern Show. Retrieved from factba.se/search#She will always be cute

[27] Zimmerman, N. (2016, October 13). Trump told 14-year-old girl he'd be dating her soon. Retrieved from thehill.com/blogs/blog-briefing-room/news/300928-trump-told-14-year-old-girl-hell-be-dating-her-soon

[28] Mathis-Lilley, B. (2016, April 06). The Daily Show Found a Video of Donald Trump Talking About His 1-Year-Old Daughter's Breasts. Retrieved from slate.com/blogs/the_slatest/2016/04/06/video_donald_trump_on_his_one_year_old_daughter_s_brests.html

[29] Stuart, T. (2018, June 25). A Timeline of Donald Trump's Creepiness While He Owned Miss Universe. Retrieved from rollingstone.com/politics/politics-features/a-timeline-of-donald-trumps-creepiness-while-he-owned-miss-universe-191860/

[30] Romo, V. (2018, March 23). Former 'Playboy' Model Spills Details of Alleged Affair: 'Trump Tried to Pay Me.' Retrieved from npr.org/sections/thetwo-way/2018/03/23/596257288/former-playboy-model-spills-alleged-affair-details-trump-tried-to-pay-her

[31] Maza, C. (2018, June 20). Donald Trump threw Starbursts at Angela Merkel, saying "don't say I never give you anything." Retrieved from newsweek.com/donald-trump-threw-starburst-candies-angela-merkel-dont-say-i-never-give-you-987178

[32] Folley, A. (2018, June 21). Ian Bremmer: Trump tossed candy to Merkel at G-7, said 'Don't say I never give you anything.' Retrieved from thehill.com/blogs/blog-briefing-room/news/393311-ian-bremmer-trump-tossed-candy-to-merkel-during-g-7-said-dont

[33] https://www.youtube.com/watch?v=R9R2kohK050

[34] U.S. Department of Justice. Raising Awareness About Sexual Abuse: Facts and Statistics. Retrieved October 1, 2018, from nsopw.gov/(X(1)S(3tzljwxacmfade5ebjqdji20))/en-US/Education/FactsStatistics

[35] SARSSM. Sexual Assault and Rape Statistics, Laws, and Reports. Retrieved October 1, 2018, from sarsonline.org/resources-stats/reports-laws-statics

[36] Newman, S. (2017, May 12). What kind of person makes false rape accusations? Retrieved from https://qz.com/980766/the-truth-about-false-rape-accusations/

[37] Lee, M. (2016, September 26). Fact Check: Has Trump declared bankruptcy four or six times? Retrieved from washingtonpost.com/politics/2016/live-updates/general-election/real-time-fact-checking-and-analysis-of-the-first-presidential-debate/fact-check-has-trump-declared-bankruptcy-four-or-six-times

[38] Kruse, M. (2018, June 01). 'He Pretty Much Gave In to Whatever They Asked For'. Retrieved from politico.com/magazine/story/2018/06/01/donald-trump-deals-negotiation-art-of-deal-218584

[39] Lewandowski Defends Trump: 'He's the Greatest Deal-Maker Our Country's Ever Seen.' (2017, April 22). Retrieved from insider.foxnews.com/2017/04/22/corey-lewandowski-president-trump-accomplishments-first-100-days

[40] Kruse, M. (2018, June 01). 'He Pretty Much Gave In to Whatever They Asked For'.

[41] Groden, C. (2015, August 20). Donald Trump Would Be Richer If He'd Have Invested in Index Funds. Retrieved from fortune.com/2015/08/20/donald-trump-index-funds

[42] Kruse, M. (2018, June 01). 'He Pretty Much Gave In to Whatever They Asked For.'

[43] Murphy, Bernice. (2010). "You Space Bastard! You Killed My Pines!" Back to the Future, Nostalgia and the Suburban Dream. 49-62.

[44] Leinberger, C., & Leinberger, L. (2014, February 28). The Top 12 Movies About Urbanism. Retrieved from nextcity.org/daily/entry/the-top-12-movies-about-urbanism

[45] Factbase. (2018, August 13). Transcript - Remarks: Donald Trump Delivers a Speech at a Fundraiser in Utica, NY - August 13, 2018. Retrieved from factba.se/transcript/donald-trump-remarks-fundraiser-utica-ny-august-13-2018

[46] Republican Debate: Read the Transcript of the Primetime Debate. (2015, August 07). Retrieved from time.com/3988276/republican-debate-primetime-transcript-full-text/

[47] Schulman, K. (2011, May 11). "The President's Speech" at the White House Correspondents' Dinner. Retrieved from obamawhitehouse.archives.gov/blog/2011/05/01/president-s-speech-white-house-correspondents-dinner

[48] Anonymous. (2018, September 05). I Am Part of the Resistance Inside the Trump Administration. Retrieved from nytimes.com/2018/09/05/opinion/trump-white-house-anonymous-resistance.html

[49] FandangoNOW Extras. (2014, March 11). Back to the Future Part III Deleted Scene - The Tannen Gang Kill Marshall Strickland (1990) Movie HD. Retrieved from youtube.com/watch?v=2RYb7GHWuL4

[50] Grynbaum, M. (2017, February 17). Trump Calls the News Media the 'Enemy of the American People.' Retrieved from nytimes.com/2017/02/17/business/trump-calls-the-news-media-the-enemy-of-the-people.html

[51] Wilson, J. (2018, June 14). Doxxing, assault, death threats: The new dangers facing U.S. journalists covering extremism. Retrieved from theguardian.com/world/2018/jun/14/doxxing-assault-death-threats-the-new-dangers-facing-us-journalists-covering-extremism

[52] Diamond, J. (2016, January 24). Donald Trump could 'shoot somebody and not lose voters' - CNNPolitics. Retrieved from cnn.com/2016/01/23/politics/donald-trump-shoot-somebody-support/

[53] Hu, E. (2017, September 22). Kim Jong Un Issues Statement on Trump: 'A Frightened Dog Barks Louder.' Retrieved from npr.org/sections/thetwo-way/2017/09/21/552756716/kim-jong-un-issues-statement-on-trump-a-frightened-dog-barks-louder

[54] Flores, R. (2016, July 21). Mike Pence introduces himself to GOP in convention speech. Retrieved from cbsnews.com/news/mike-pence-introduces-himself-to-gop-in-convention-speech/

[55] Federal News Service transcript. (2016, September 8). Mike Pence Remarks at Reagan Library. Retrieved from c-span.org/video/?c4619417/mike-pence-remarks-reagan-library

[56] Smith, D. (2016, October 04). Tim Kaine v Mike Pence: What to know about the vice-presidential candidates. Retrieved from https://www.theguardian.com/us-news/2016/oct/04/mike-pence-tim-kaine-facts-vp-debate-trump-clinton

[57] Alberta, T. (2018, January/February). How Donald Trump Came Between Mike Pence and Jeff Flake. Retrieved from politico.com/magazine/story/2018/01/03/mike-pence-jeff-flake-republican-party-friendship-216208

www.ingramcontent.com/pod-product-compliance
Lightning Source LLC
Chambersburg PA
CBHW062124040426
42337CB00044B/4067